Another Visit to the Mountaintop

A History of Mt. Lake Park, Maryland
1881 - 1921

George Cowgill

Big Pasture Publishing, LLC

Email: BigPasturePub@gmail.com

Copyright © 2023 George Cowgill

All rights reserved.

ISBN-13: 979-8-218-18667-8

ACKNOWLEDGEMENTS

Many people have been generous and provided material for this history of Mountain Lake Park. I'd like to thank everyone that opened their doors and their vaults to provide guidance, photos, and stories. This includes: Marilyn Blake, Bob Boal, Kevin Callis, Barbara Chesley, Carolyn S. Corley, Stephanie Cowgill, Steve Cowgill, J.Hornor Davis, IV, Dave and Mimi Degrafft, Bill and Tammy Ewing, Linda Fike, Elizabeth Gilbert, Sarah Haynes, Carolyn Henderson, Martha Kahl, Kathy Malone, Steve Maxwell, Bob Moore, Jenny and Jim Neville, Walter Pollard, Jr., Edward Poling, Beverly Railey Robinson, Laura Robinson, Diana Runyan, Don Sincell, Katharine Smith, Sally Steyer, Richard Tritt, and Karen Wooddell. I would also like to posthumously recognize the work of Mary I. Love; her earlier research paved the way for a book such as this.

DEDICATION

To my wife, Ellen, for her patience and support.

CONTENTS

	Acknowledgments	ii
1	Introduction - Guidebook	1
2	Before The Beginning	13
3	The Founders & The Big Idea	15
4	The Importance of the Railroad	21
5	Post Office, Boardwalk & Pilgrims' Rest	27
6	Getting About	33
7	Chautauqua Assemblies	37
8	Time Line of Events 1881-1921	72
9	Black People of Mt. Lake Park	74
10	Association Buildings	79
11	The Hotels & Boarding Houses	100
12	The "Cottages"	128
13	The Mountain Lake	139
14	Crystal Spring	148
15	Wintertime	152
16	Electric, Water, & Sewers, Oh My!	159
17	Calamities	165
18	More on the Founders	173
19	What Happened?	178

A word about the photographs in this book. Unless otherwise stated, the images are courtesy of the Mt. Lake Park Historical Association. Many of the people in the photos are unidentified. To avoid repetition, only those that are known are identified in the captions. The images used in this book are largely unaltered; no artificial intelligence was used to generate these photos.

1 - INTRODUCTION – THE GUIDEBOOK

There are many possible approaches to introducing a book on the history of a place. One could write a lengthy introduction/overview; describing the highlights of the area, the dry facts about a natural resource, or battle, or the importance of a particular type of commerce. This book is a picture-oriented book, and Mt. Lake was formed and influenced by visitors who traveled to the Park. So, we will start with a travel guidebook, presenting information the reader might need if they were planning a trip to the Park just after the turn of the century, in the hopes that this will provide a bit of orientation.

The focus of this book is to inform readers about the people, places and events of Mt. Lake and offer views of the Park not published before. There will be names and dates, and a sufficient number of sensational stories to keep the reader engaged, and most important of all, efforts to convey the nature of the origin of the summer resort that came to be known as Mt. Lake Park. We can say "came to be known" because the first news references to the project were named "Meadow Lake Park", although this working term was quickly discarded.[1]

After much study of the subject, there are two overarching points worth highlighting about the history of the Park- it was strictly conceived as a religious summer resort, to be used less than three months during the year, and secondly, it succeeded, though not necessarily financially, far beyond the founders' imaginations. Shortly after its creation, the Park evolved into a "Daughter Chautauqua", one of the biggest of any of the "Chautauqua towns", modeled after the "Mother Chautauqua" in New York.

For those of us who live in sleepy Mt. Lake today, it is hard to imagine the level of activity during those 10 or so summer weeks, with thousands of visitors, hundreds of speakers and performers, large conferences attracting up to one thousand people each, religious camp meetings, summer school classes, and all the Hotels, Boarding Houses, Cottages, Dining Halls, and (acceptable) Amusements needed to support them all.

The season would start in earnest around the middle of June, and run full-on until August 30th, usually ending with a grand fireworks display.

Just as quickly, as the calendar rolled over to September, the visitors, performers, and preachers would leave, the summer school students would graduate, the hotels would shut down, the trains would no longer stop at the Park, and, once there was electricity, the electric to the resort would be turned off! [2]

In the early years, the Park in December was an ominous portend to what would happen 50 years later, when the visitors ceased to come at all. There were several factors that contributed to the decline of Mt. Lake and these factors will be explored in due time.

To provide a quick glimpse of Mt. Lake Park, the "Mountain Chautauqua" in its heyday, we next present **a 10 page guidebook**, modeled after popular tour guide books of today, to give the reader a sense of what they might experience in the Park just after 1900. The reader is encouraged to review the guidebook and imagine, as if they were planning a summer visit to Mt. Lake Park. Although the guidebook has been formulated from items before 1906, all the places, people and activities did exist and they will be explored in more detail later in this book.

1906 Map of Mt. Lake Park, Maryland[3]

1906 Map of Mt. Lake Park, Maryland

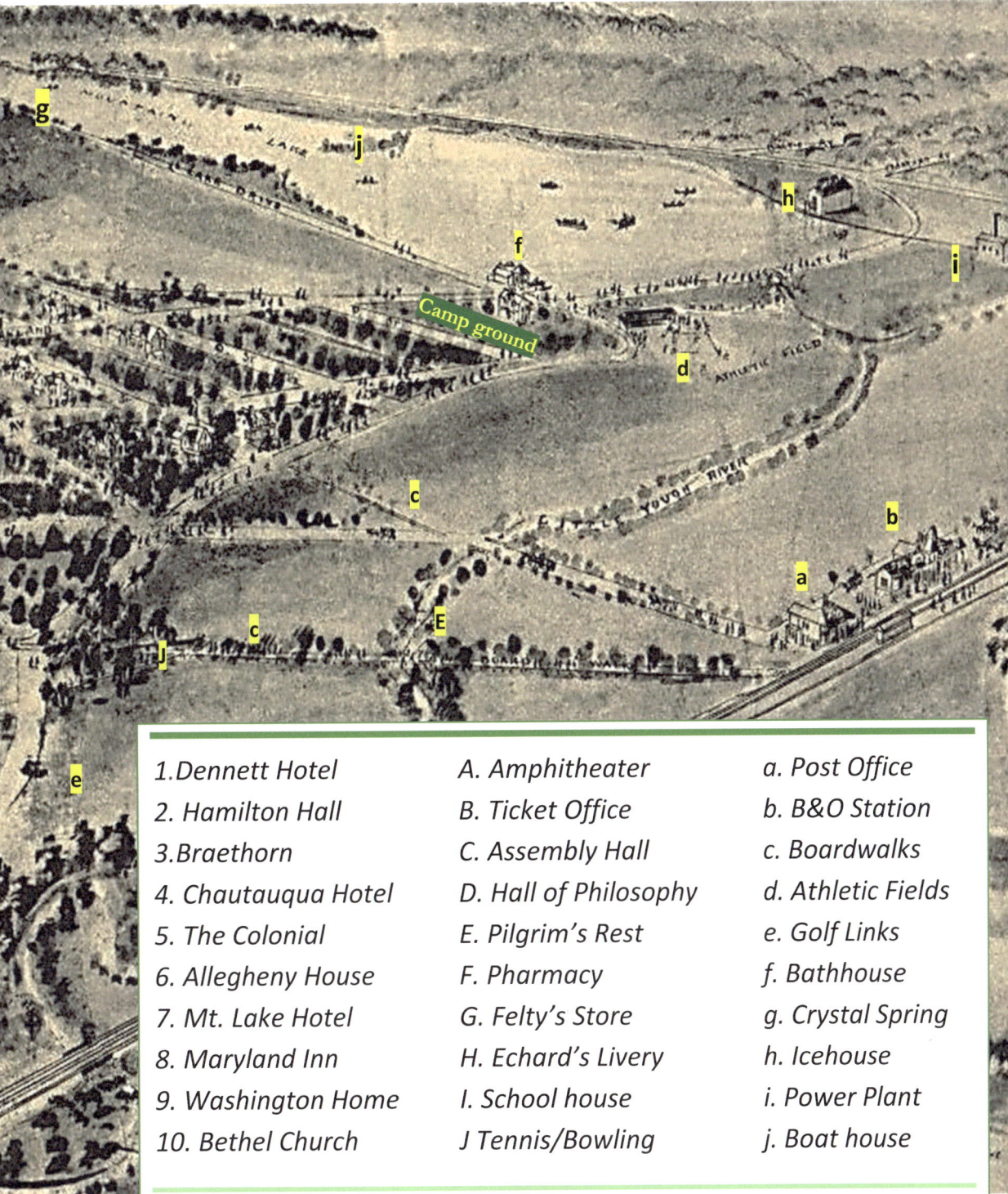

1. Dennett Hotel	A. Amphitheater	a. Post Office
2. Hamilton Hall	B. Ticket Office	b. B&O Station
3. Braethorn	C. Assembly Hall	c. Boardwalks
4. Chautauqua Hotel	D. Hall of Philosophy	d. Athletic Fields
5. The Colonial	E. Pilgrim's Rest	e. Golf Links
6. Allegheny House	F. Pharmacy	f. Bathhouse
7. Mt. Lake Hotel	G. Felty's Store	g. Crystal Spring
8. Maryland Inn	H. Echard's Livery	h. Icehouse
9. Washington Home	I. School house	i. Power Plant
10. Bethel Church	J Tennis/Bowling	j. Boat house

Your Visitor Guidebook to Mt. Lake Park, Maryland
Summer of 1906

Getting There

If you are travelling farther than a couple hours by horse or carriage, the most convenient way to get to the "Park" is via train. Because the Park is located on the main line of the B&O railroad, there are usually 3 trains daily, each way, that stop at the park from Mid-June through September 1st. Because the park operates a "closed gate" (no commerce on the Sabbath), the trains don't stop on Sundays. If you need to catch a train on Sunday, you will need to make arrangements in either Oakland or Deer Park.

For special events, such as one of the big conferences, or the big draws on the Amphitheater's Chautauqua Platform, the B&O offers special excursion trains. These trains often have reduced fares. Look for handbills or check with your B&O agent for excursion train schedules and prices.

Express Baggage wagons will meet you at the station (**b** on the map) and transport you to your Hotel or Boarding house.

B&O Station, Mt. Lake

If you are planning a longer stay and you wish to bring your own horse and carriage, you can transport these on the rail. Check with your B&O agent for details. There are 3 nearby livery's that can meet your rig at the station and board your horses.

The Schedule

The Park events usually kick off in early July and run through G.A.R. (Grand Army of the Republic) day at the end of August. Be sure to check the schedule in the Mountain Chautauqua newsletter. Details are provided on the camp meeting schedule, the summer schools, and the "talent" booked for the Amphitheater.

Some restrictions

The Park is operated as a religious Methodist resort and, to keep the park free of immoral influences, the following restrictions are enforced at all times:

- No Alcohol allowed
- No Dancing
- No Card Playing
- No Gambling
- Strict observance of the Lord's Day

There are severe penalties for violating these restrictions and they are strictly enforced. We are sure you will enjoy your time in the Park, free from these dangerous influences.

Getting around

Once you have arrived in Mt. Lake, you are but a short walk from most everything. There are extensive boardwalks if the weather should turn inclement. The town has been laid out with wide avenues that make carriage rides most pleasant.

Stables available in the Park

Hacks operate from early morning until well into the evening, excepting Sundays. Their farecards are clearly displayed in each cab so as to avoid any temptation of "over charging".

A hack can be rented for an excursion, with prices varying depending on the size of the carriage and your preference of wooden or rubber tires.

Excursions can be planned for group visits to the many nearby scenic sites, such as the Boiling Spring, Swallow Falls, and the big hotels such as the Deer Park Hotel or the Oakland Hotel.

Rent a cart or bring your own Horse & cart on the train.

1906 Travel Guide

Things to Do

The highlight of most folk's visit, besides simply relaxing, is partaking in the numerous assembly programs that allow one to become more informed and enlightened, in a devout atmosphere, free from tempting influences.

Mountain Chautauqua Summer Schools

The Park will provide a full Chautauqua curriculum, led by Superintendent W.L. Davis and Dean James Henry Morgan. Dr. Davis will have overall charge of the program and Dr. Morgan is Dean of the summer schools. Dr. Morgan is a distinguished professor from Dickinson College and he will oversee the following courses and lectures:

Dean J.H. Morgan

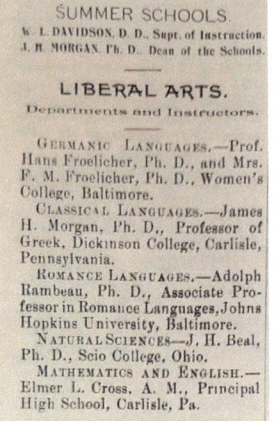

SUMMER SCHOOLS.
W. L. DAVIDSON, D. D., Supt. of Instruction.
J. H. MORGAN, Ph. D., Dean of the Schools.

LIBERAL ARTS.
Departments and Instructors.

GERMANIC LANGUAGES.—Prof. Hans Froelicher, Ph. D., and Mrs. F. M. Froelicher, Ph. D., Women's College, Baltimore.
CLASSICAL LANGUAGES.—James H. Morgan, Ph. D., Professor of Greek, Dickinson College, Carlisle, Pennsylvania.
ROMANCE LANGUAGES.—Adolph Rambeau, Ph. D., Associate Professor in Romance Languages, Johns Hopkins University, Baltimore.
NATURAL SCIENCES—J. H. Beal, Ph. D., Scio College, Ohio.
MATHEMATICS AND ENGLISH.—Elmer L. Cross, A. M., Principal High School, Carlisle, Pa.

FINE ARTS.
Departments and Instructors.

PAINTING.—Miss Jennie White, Madisonville, Ohio.
MUSIC.—W. H. Pontius, Dubuque, Iowa.
ELOCUTION.—Miss Julia A. Orum, Principal of Philadelphia and Mt. Lake Park School of Elocution, 1520 Chestnut street, Philadelphia, Pa.
PHYSICAL CULTURE.—Miss Lydia J. Newcomb, Bethlehem, Pa.
KINDERGARTEN.—Miss Susan P. Pollock, Principal Froebel Kindergarten, 1426 Q St., Washington, D. C.
AMATEUR PHOTOGRAPHY.—Prof. A. A. Line, Carlisle, Pa.
STENOGRAPHY, TYPEWRITING & BOOKKEEPING.—D. D. Mueller, Bartlett's Business College, Cincinnati, Ohio.

The corps of instructors includes some of the most well-known men and women of letters. Tuition has been fixed at the low rate of $3.00 in most of the departments for the full term of three weeks.[4] The class lectures are held in the Assembly Hall (**C**), the Amphitheater (**A**) and the Hall of Philosophy (**D**) School supplies can be purchased at the bookstore, near the Ticket Office (**B**)

Assembly Camp Meetings

Each year, thousands of "pilgrims" flock to the Park, to hear the best sermons anywhere. Although some of the most riveting preachers, such as Rev. John Thompson and "Addie" Sherman, have passed on, the Park is still fortunate to have a full stable of devout lecturers and missionaries on hand. In past years, there have been upwards of 500 preachers and evangelists in attendance.[5] The Summer Assembly has and ever will afford an undenominational headquarters for the many and growing movements in and between the churches.[6]

1906 Travel Guide

The Assembly Hall (Left) and Tabernacle (Right)

The famous Bashford Amphitheater, built in 1900.

The main services are held in the 5000 seat Amphitheater (New Auditorium, **A** on map) and the Assembly Hall & Tabernacle. (Old Auditorium, **C** on Map)

Inside the Bashford Amphitheater

7

Chautauqua Assembly Platform

Each year, Dr. W.L. Davidson works to assemble the best "talent", of a national reputation for your enjoyment. In previous years, speakers such as Gov. Lee of Virginia, "Captain Jack", the poet scout, William Jennings Bryan, and Dr. Sam Jones have graced the Platform. Dr. Davidson always manages to secure the best acts found on the Chautauqua circuit, such as the Shepardson Lady Quartette, Charles Carter the magician, and Stanley Krebs and his lectures with experiments.

This year promises to be no exception, and with 5 attractions daily and season passes costing only $4.00, it is truly a bargain. The main attractions perform in the Bashford Amphitheater (**A**) and smaller lectures are located in the Hall of Philosophy (**D**) and the Assembly Hall (**C**). Tickets can be purchase at the ticket office (**B**) in front of the Amphitheater.

1906 Travel Guide

Where to Stay

There are nearly thirty boarding houses and hotels operating in season in the Park. These places tend to fill up early, so be sure to contact the proprietor well before the season starts. Rooms and apartments can be rented with or without table board. Many of the hotels and boarding houses advertise in the big city papers and in the Mountain Chautauqua magazine.

> **ALLEGHENEY HOUSE,**
> **MOUNTAIN LAKE PARK, MARYLAND.**
> **MRS. L. F. BULLARD, Proprietor**
>
> A charming summer home, choicely located, comfortably furnished, and delightfully kept. Special plans for the promotion of the pleasure and convenience of the guests for this season are being wrought out. The extensive improvements made at the Park will make a sojourn there during the summer peculiarly enjoyable. The healthfulness and other natural advantages of this unexcelled resort will be supplemented by unusual social, literary and moral attractions.
> The Allegheney House will be opened at an early date, and will remain open until October 15th. Sufferers from the tortures of "hay fever" by coming to the Park before the time of attack and remaining until October, will escape its ravages for the season. Parties desiring accommodations had better apply early. Address Mrs. Bullard until May 15th, at Bridgeport, Ohio.

From the Mountain Top Messenger

Here is a sampling of the hotels and boarding houses with a reference to the birds-eye view map found in the beginning of this guidebook:

- **Overlook Hotel**, formerly Dennett Hotel, **(1)** on map. Full-service hotel operated by Mrs. L.B.C. List (formerly of the Loch Lynn Hotel) Price level: $$
- **Hamilton Hall** (formerly Faith Hall), **(2)** on map. Full-service Hotel. Price level $$
- **The Columbian**, near **(2)** on map. Full-service hotel operated by the Lewis family. Livery on site. Price level: $$
- **Braethorn Inn**, near the grove, **(3)** on map. Boarding house with table board available. Price level $$$
- **Chautauqua Hotel** (formally Grace Cottage) **(4)** on map. Full-service Hotel, just across from the Amphitheater. Price level: $$
- **The Colonial (5)** on map. Boarding house, operated by the Weimer family. Price level: $
- **Allegheny House (6)** on map. Boarding house, operated by the Mrs. Bullard. Price level: $$
- **Mt. Lake Park Hotel (7)** on map. The park's original full-service hotel, continuously operated since 1882. Price level: $$$
- **Maryland Inn (8)** on map. Boarding House, 1 block from the Amphitheater. Price level: $$

1906 Travel Guide

Tents can be rented at a reasonable rate for the week, month, or season. (see Map area labeled **"Campground"**, near the bathhouse (**f.** on the map.)) Tent floors can be erected by carpenters, they advertise in the Mountain Chautauqua Magazine. Tent furniture can be rented at Richardson's Furniture Bazaar, located in the Park.

There are a limited number of cottages available for rent for the entire season. These cottages usually come furnished with everything needed, but some require the rental of furniture for the summer. The park superintendent keeps close tabs on which cottages are available and can help make arrangements for domestic help if needed.

If you come for a visit and enjoy a summer in the Park as much as everyone else, you might want to buy a lot and build your own cottage. Lots can be had for as little as $50 and local carpenters can erect your very own cottage before next season.

Good Eats

The fresh mountain air can stimulate a big appetite; there are number of places in the Park serving "good eats" morning, noon, and night. If you are staying at a boarding house or hotel, board can be included at a weekly rate. When you are out and about, lunch can be had at one of the refreshment stands that operate in the grove(near **C** on map), and there are dining halls (near **4** on map) nearby. There is never a shortage of fresh baked goods in the Park, as several bakeries operate in the park in season. For those

Refreshment Stand

From the Mountain Top Messenger

camping or staying in a home rented by the week such as "Cozy Row", groceries can be delivered from Felty's (**G**), or P.T. Garthwright's store. The big farms in nearby "pleasant valley" ensure a steady supply of fresh vegetables, meat, and dairy products.

Getting Mail and Newspapers

The post office is located next door to the train station (**a** on the map). Mail is received 3 times daily and, with the use of the wide boardwalks, (**c.** on the map) it is always a pleasant stroll to check for mail. A small supply store is located in the post office and one- cent stamped postcards, with beautiful views of the Park, can be purchased there. All the big city newspapers can be purchased, same day, at the post office store.

1906 Travel Guide

Fun and games

In addition to the camp meetings, the Summer Schools, Chautauqua Performers, and croquet, there are many healthy outdoor activities to be enjoyed in the Park. **Note: these activities, are strictly forbidden on Sunday.**

Bathing

The mountain lake provides a refreshing place to bath during the summer season. Bathing Suits and Life Buoys can be rented by the hour. Prices range up to 35 cents per hour.

Boating is always relaxing at the lake. Boats can be rented by the hour or by the day, with choices of specially built row boats and canoes available.

Horses are available for hire, at the livery stables, and riding lessons can be provided. All rented horses are outfitted with blankets, saddles, and bridles. Check with one of the livery stables to schedule a ride.

Fishing

There are plenty of fish to be had in the mountain lake, with a good supply of trout early in the season. Anglers can be outfitted at the Mt. Lake Boathouse.

Picnics at the Crystal Springs

There may be no more pleasant way to spend an afternoon than pitching a picnic at the Crystal Springs. The spring is known for its healthful waters and the quiet pool that collects the spring water. It is located (**g** on the map) just north of the lake.

Bowling and Tennis can be played at the Clubhouse. (**J** on map) The bowling alley is a recent addition and has been very well frequented. Bowling Balls are provided.

Tennis matches are now a favorite activity. Interest in the annual Mt. Lake Park tennis tournament continues to grow, with crowds each year surpassing the previous summer.

Golf

The golf links are a new feature of the park (**e** on map); the golf course is maintained by the Mt. Lake Park Hotel. Please contact the hotel staff to engage in a round of golf.

Plan an Excursion

Carriage rides are available for picnic trips to several scenic sites.

MUDDY CREEK FALLS—near Mountain Lake Park, Md.

11

1906 Travel Guide

Should the need arise, the Park Pharmacy (F on map) is open from June-September. Dr.'s Laughlin and McComas visit the Park as well.

The recently built (Bethel) M.E. Church (10 on map) offers Sunday Services.

> **REST, QUIET, HEALTH FOR EVERYBODY.**
>
> MOUNTAIN LAKE PARK is a tract of eight hundred acres in extent—forest and glade. No one is compelled to anything to which his taste does not incline him. In so large a territory everyone can have his choice of place and occupation. Only those things are forbidden which would tend to disturb the peace and rest of the community.
> For further information, and for illustrated descriptive circulars, send to
>
> JOHN M. DAVIS, Superintendent,

From a Mt. Lake Park Marketing Flyer, ca. 1884.

This concludes our example travel guide to Mt. Lake Park, as you might have experienced it around 1906. The map used in the guidebook may be referenced in subsequent chapters. **There are more than 145 historical structures remaining in the Park**. We now take a moment and identify the buildings and places identified in the map legend that are no longer in existence, or abandoned.

Remaining Structures

1. Dennett Hotel	*A. Amphitheater*	*a. Post Office*
2. Hamilton Hall	B. Ticket Office	*b. B&O Station*
3. Braethorn	C. Assembly Hall	*c. Boardwalks*
4. Chautauqua Hotel	*D. Hall of Philosophy*	*d. Athletic Fields*
5. The Colonial	*E. Pilgrim's Rest*	*e. Golf Links*
6. Allegheny House	F. Pharmacy	*f. Bathhouse*
7. Mt. Lake Hotel	G. Felty's Store	g. Crystal Spring
8. Maryland Inn	*H. Echard's Livery*	*h. Icehouse*
9. Washington Home	I. School house	*i. Power Plant*
10. Bethel Church	J Tennis/Bowling	*j. Boat house*

Those places in light gray have been torn down; the Crystal Spring still flows but it is abandoned. The B & O station, school house, and bowling alley exist but have been re-purposed. And, of course, the Mountain Lake itself is but a marshy lakebed. As we wander through the history of the park in the succeeding chapters, we will learn much more about these places and the people of the "Mountaintop".

2 - BEFORE THE BEGINNING

"...the entire region was grazing ground..." - **John Davis' 1859 description.**

As we start to tease out the history of Mountain Lake Park, it is useful to get a sense of what the area was like prior to 1881. Going back in time, the area which would become the summer resort was woodland, broken up by "glades" or natural meadows. This area was traversed by Native Americans, who had camps in the southern and central parts of what is now Garrett County. We might consider them the first "summer visitors" to the area, as it appears that they had the practical sense to follow the buffalo through the area in the summer, camping at springs and along rivers, but then migrated back to lower elevations before winter set in.[1]

Excerpt from Map annotated by John Grant Courtesy of Garrett County Historical Society.

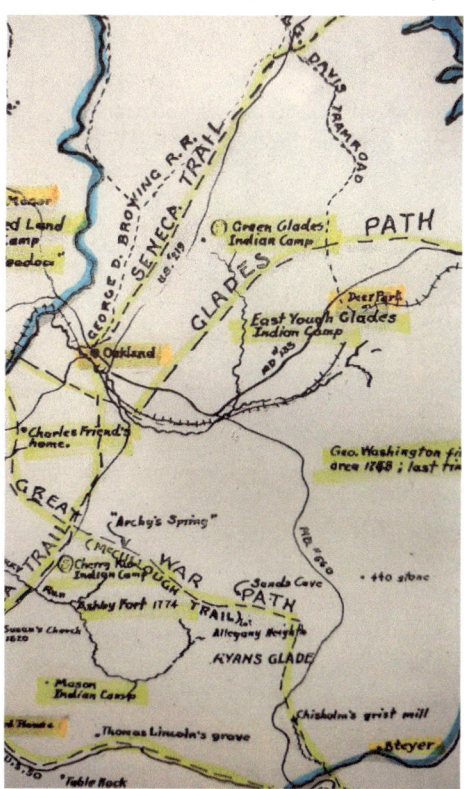

Seneca Trail near Oakland and Mt. Lake from the Glades Star Vol. 10 No. 8, 2004. Photo by Carolyn White.

Garrett county had some major trails intersecting in the county, established in the distant past; these include the Glades path, Seneca trail, and McCullough's trail (also known as the Great War Path). By 1860, the area that would be the "Park", was known as "John Hoye's Big Pasture"; it was part of John Hoye's larger tract of land known as the "Western Canal Convention".[2] Because of the nutritious manna grass, which grew over five feet tall in the glades, the area provided good grazing for cattle.

Before the Beginning

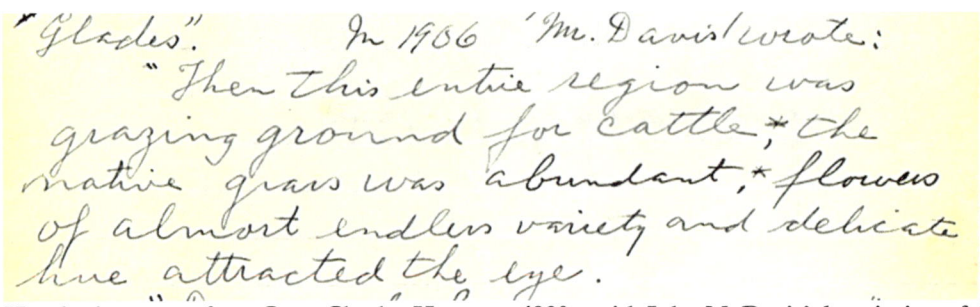

Handwritten note from Capt. Charles Hoye, ca. 1930s, with John M. Davis' description of the area. From the Hoye Collection, Georgetown University Archives

Initially these cattle were managed on open range and subsequently the area of Hoye's Pasture was fenced. A Mr. George White leased Hoye's pasture and fenced it in.[3] The railroad had arrived in 1852, but it merely rolled through the woods and pasture as it ran from Deer Park to Oakland. The Deer Park Hotel, operated by the B&O railroad, had been built in 1873, and saw great success catering to the prominent society from the East, offering them a respite from the summer doldrums experienced in the big eastern cities.[4] Oakland was the nearest actual town at that time, with hotels, banks, stores, and churches. To get a glimpse of what newly-minted Garrett County was like before 1880, we can review a story told by Mr. John M. Davis about herding cattle in 1859, when the area was still part of Allegheny County. John M. Davis would later figure prominently in the organizing of Mt. Lake Park.

This story was written down by Capt. Charles Hoye, likely in the 1930s, and is Mr. John M. Davis's tale (told in 1906) of his cattle operation in the area:

"In the summer of 1859, I herded 600 head of cattle on what is known as the Harrington Creek glade. At the time between 1000 to 2000 cattle were annually pastured within the radius of 10 miles; deer were numerous, speckled trout could be caught in almost any of the streams. Farmers were few and it was thought to be useless to try to raise wheat or corn."

Rev. John M. Davis

Mr. Davis continues:

"When a boy, I wholesaled a drove of cattle to some eastern buyers, delivered the stock to Harrisburg, Pennsylvania, received the proceeds in cash, amounting to about $5000. I returned on horseback, carrying the money with me, spent a night with my Mother in Somerset County (Pennsylvania), continued my journey to find my Father, who was buying cattle near St. George or Beverly, Virginia (now West Virginia). I passed through Cranberry Summit (now Terra Alta), to Aurora. Before reaching the latter place, night overtook me. I thought the dark hollows near Aurora were the 'spookiest' places I had ever seen. I suppose had it not been that I was carrying the proceeds of a drove of cattle in my pocket I would have thought but little of the darkness or the wildness of the country."

In short, these descriptions sound similar to cattle operations much further west. But just as the railroad began to make its mark on the area, Garrett County *was* the west.

3 - THE FOUNDERS AND THE BIG IDEA

"Mountain Lake Park was founded on Idealism and Mountain Air" – quote from Mary Love, Author of <u>Once Upon a Mountaintop</u>.

To trace the origins of Mountain Lake Park, we must review activities in the late 1870s in Moundsville, West Virginia. Summer religious camp meetings were held at the "camp ground" in Moundsville and thousands of people came to hear the religious preaching and to socialize. Dr. Logan Carr, one of the "early birds" to Mt. Lake, said about Moundsville.[1] *"The people came in buggies, in saddles, on foot and on railroad excursions.* (They also came on steamboats down from Wheeling.) *On Sundays, the meeting grounds became a vast mass of moving people, happy people having a gay time. But among these people were those who demanded a '"closed gate" Sunday in order that their Sabbath be regarded more as a day of quiet worship than a day of carefree frivolity. Their minority demand for restrictions, however, was overruled."*

Camp Grounds, Moundsville, WV, which operated an "open gate" on Sunday.

Tabernacle Moundsville, WV

Thus, because of the denied request for quiet Sundays in Moundsville, a plan was hatched to create a separate religious resort, that would operate with a "closed gate" on Sundays, and also have other restrictions on alcohol use, dancing, card playing, and the like. In 1881, the men behind this plan, mostly from Wheeling, WV, began the search for a site in Western Maryland, which was located in the West Virginia Conference area of the Methodist Episcopal Church.

> "The object of this Association shall be to establish a Summer Resort, founded upon Christian principles, and designed to afford opportunities for Religious Literary Instruction and healthful recreation."

From Article 2, Mt. Lake Park Association Charter

The Founders and The Big Idea

In September 1881, the 'search party' arrived in Oakland, Maryland via train. J.A. Enlow, who was present during the search, picks up the story:[2]

During the autumn of 1881 there was a company of men came to Oakland, namely: Rev. C. P. Masden, Major J. C. Alderson, Rev. Snodgrass and C. W. Conner, all of Wheeling, and Rev. E. W. Regan (Ryan), of Morgantown, West Va. Rev. Benjamin Ison was then pastor of the Oakland M. E. church. He and Rev. John M. Davis were called into a conference to aid in selecting a suitable location for a Christian summer resort. The first day they inspected the tract of land known as "William and Mary," lying northwest of Oakland and along the Youghiogheny River. (Note: this is out near the present day Oakland golf course.) This tract of land was thought fine for the purpose but did not extend to the limits of the Baltimore and Ohio railroad.

The following day they went to examine the land belonging to the Hoye estate and beginning on its western border about a mile from Oakland. J.A. Enlow joined the party with his little saddle horse and which Rev. Regan (Ryan) accepted and rode from where the party had left their spring wagon at or about the point where Hamilton Hall now stands (this would be on Deer Park Ave.), and rode south to the Baltimore and Ohio tracks, while the others inspected the land lying to the east and north and which at that time was all woods. When the party had assembled at the point where the wagon had been left, Rev. Regan with much stress and emphasis said, "Brethren, this is foreordained for the place we are seeking," to which all agreed.

Rev. C. P. Masden and Major Alderson were designated as a committee to wait on W. D. Hoye, one of the heirs, who lived where the Weber green houses are now located and who informed them the Mr. George Smith, of Bedford, Pa., was their agent. The following day these men went to see Mr. Smith and they contracted with him for the purchase of the Hoye interest in five hundred acres. Robert H. Gordon, of Cumberland, owned 300 acres adjoining the Hoye property, and upon their return from Bedford the party stopped in Cumberland and purchased the Gordon land, thus giving them eight hundred acres in all, with nearly a mile and a half of rail road frontage.

A survey of the property was later made by Mr. John Harned, who was assisted in the work by H. Lowe, W.D. Burton and James A. Enlow. The survey started at the double white oaks on which the Military Lots hinged. These trees stood on what is now known as the Dennett road and running parallel with the State road leading to Oakland.

J. A. Enlow's detailed account of the 1881 scouting, purchase, and survey of the tracts of land that would become Mt. Lake Park. Mr. Enlow and many of the men mentioned in this account would have prominent roles in the Park Association.

At the request of Mountain Lake Park Association of Garrett County this deed was recorded Oct. 2 1881.

Preamble to one of the Deeds for MLP

The Founders and The Big Idea

Some of the "Founders". Rev. C. P. Masden, Major J. C. Alderson, C.W. Conner, Rev. Charles W. Baldwin, Dr. John Goucher, Rev. John M. Davis, S.L. Allen

The idea was to create a religious resort, where people could enjoy the then-new trend of taking a vacation, but to ensure an environment that didn't offer too many temptations, as many religious people, such as these Methodists, were a bit wary of leisure time.[3] These "founders" were at the far-end of the religious spectrum as they wanted to, and indeed they did, place wide ranging restrictions on what was allowable in their new "Park".

The Methodist ministers went to great lengths to try to ensure the new park would be free from "immoral" influences; this was spelled out in their Association charter:

> *"The Board of Directors shall make regulations regarding a due observance of the Sabbath day; and the buying, selling, or using intoxicating liquor as a beverage, card playing, dancing and all immoral practices are strictly prohibited."*

These prohibitions can be traced to the "Amusement Prohibition" found in the Methodist Book of Discipline in the late 19th century. With very similar language, the Church spelled out all the same "amusements" and prohibited them.[4] The church also specified what consequences might be meted out for a first (1st time, visit from minister), second, and third infraction. Eventually, a person could get excommunicated after a few infractions.

The Mt. Lake Park Association took the punishment aspect to an entirely new level, when they spelled out in each lot deed, that violations to the park regulations could result in the loss of your house!

Ethel Turney, an early resident of Mt. Lake quipped, *"with those bylaws, why, you didn't even chew chewing gum, now I mean it!*[5]

This might be a good time to mention how difficult the enforcement of these prohibitions can be, as, at the same time the Association was purchasing the land for the new "Park", one of their number, Major J.C. Alderson, bought 213 acres just across the

At the request of Joseph O. Alderson & others this deed was recorded Sept. 30, 1881 at 9 3/4 o'clock A.M.

Preamble to J.C. Alderson's deed to the land that would become Loch Lynn.

railroad tracks from the park property. The town that grew up there, Loch Lynn Heights, was known as a "wide open" town, where frivolity and card playing were not only tolerated, they were oft-times encouraged. So, if a person wanted to "Sin", all they had to do was walk over to Loch Lynn. Hence the phase, ***"If you want to sin, go to Loch Lynn, but for Jesus' sake stay in Mt. Lake."*** Human nature being what it is, Loch Lynn grew right alongside Mt. Lake and was a very popular place.

Casino, with swimming pool, Loch Lynn Heights, Loch Lynn Hotel on left. Hitching Post in front of casino says "To Sebold's Livery" Courtesy Cumberland County History Museum, A.A. Line Collection

After the scouting party locked in their purchases of 800 Acres, it is surprising how fast things moved. After formally starting in September 9 of 1881, they had, within the next few months.[6]

- Scouted for Park Location (ca. Sept 10, 1881)
- Formed Association in W.V. (Sept 17, 1881)
- Formed Committee for "title to land" (Sept 19, 1881)
- Purchased two tracts of land (ca. Sept 27, 1881)

18

- Established Initial Agreements with B&O (ca. Oct. 2,1881)
- Engaged Augustus Faul for Park design (ca. Oct. 2, 1881, completed in May of 1882, cost $900)
- Formed Association in Maryland (ca. Oct. 8, 1881)
- 1st Excursion Train Announced (October 1881)
- 1st Excursion Trains and Lot sales (Nov. 1881 & May 18, 1882)
- Built a temporary dam on Broadford Run (for Ice Harvesting) (Jan. 1882)
- Built an initial Railroad Depot (March-April 1882)
- Made Plans for first buildings (March 23, 1882) ((Old)Auditorium, Post Office, Hotel)

In January of 1882, a temporary dam had been built across Broadford Run, the objective was to create a small lake or pond so that ice might be harvested for the inaugural season[7]. In the fall of 1882, Mr. Burley would construct a more permanent dam, this would form the initial Mountain Lake, which would comprise approximately 20 acres. Perhaps the biggest driver of the lake construction was the need for ice; the founders also recognized the potential for recreation.

Recalling that first summer of 1882, Mrs. Rachael Laughlin said,[8] *"The cottages were scattered and the tents were plentiful."*

By the end of the summer of 1882, public buildings, a hotel, a boarding house, and a number of cottages had been erected:

LOT HOLDERS WHO HAVE ERECTED COTTAGES.
Rev. A. S. Hank, Baltimore,
J. C. Alderson, Wheeling, W. Va.,
C. H. Beale, Brook County, W. Va.,
Rev. C. P. Masden, Scranton, Pennsylvania,
Miss Sallie Mcholin, Wheeling, W. Va,
J. M. Davis, Oakland, Md.,
S. L. Allen, Grafton, W. Va.,
Rev. T. B. Hughes, Morgantown, W. Va.,
D. C. List, Jr., Wheeling, W. Va.,
Bardall, & Weaver, Moundsville, W. Va.,
C. W. Conner, Wheeling, W. Va.,
Rev. Wm. Alexander, Moundsville, W. Va.,
Rev. J. B. Mulford, Wheeling, W. Va.,
Hon. W. H. Tarr, Welsburg, W. Va.,
Mrs. L. E. Carr, Fairmont, W. Va.,
Mrs. Geo. R. Bullard, Allegheny House,
Rev. John Thompson, Philadelphia,
Rev. L. T. Widerman, Baltimore, Md.,
Rev. E. W. Ryan, Wheeling, W. Va.,
Hon. G. W. Atkins, Wheeling, W. Va.,
A. H. Mahone, Charleston, W. Va.,
Rev. J. A. Fullerton, Moundsville, W. Va.,
Magil, Morgan & Co., Grafton, W. Va.
Rev. Jno. F. Goucher, Baltimore,
J. A. Enlow, Oakland, Md.,
T. H. Logan, Wheeling, W. Va.,
Rev. B. L. Baumgardner, Mt. Lake Park,
A. R. Sperry, Mt. Lake Park,
H. H. Van Meter, Mt. Lake Park Hotel.

Builders, Summer of 1882. From the Republican Oct. 10, 1882

We can see from this summary from the Oct. 10, 1882 edition of the Republican paper, that the Mt. Lake Park Hotel, the Allegheny Boarding house, and around 27 "Cottages" were built that first summer. It is a marvel that so much construction could happen in so little time; this points to the availability of labor, lumber, and other supplies. Also, building houses was much simpler in 1882, as there was no need to install electric, plumbing, or other modern conveniences. Building one of these early cottages was just a bit more complicated than a "barn raising". Many of the early cottages did not have interior walls as we think of them today. Ethel Turney recalled, *"They put building (tar) paper on the inside and then they wallpapered over that."* Still, when we look at the varied architecture and asymmetrical roof lines, the skill of the builders cannot be denied.

There is always considerable speculation regarding what was the first building or house completed in Mt. Lake; the information we have is not clear on this matter, any of the buildings and cottages in the above list from the summer of 1882 can be said to be "one of the first". The only other clue we can find comes from the July 1st edition of the Republican:

> *Mountain Lake Park is now ready for visitors. The hotel is completed and furnished. Mrs. Bullard's large boarding house will be ready for the season next week, and a large number of the cottages are now completed and ready for occupancy. Rev. John Thompson, manager of Pierce's Union Business cottage, Philadelphia, and Mr. Allen, of Grafton, are now in their cottages, and Rev. Masden, of Wheeling will occupy his on the 7th instant. The first religious services will be held Sunday, 9th, inst., under the direction of Rev. Thompson. The hour of meeting will be given in our next issue. Rev. John M. Davis deserves great praise for the manner in which he has pushed forward the work at the Park. Few thought last fall that near forty cottages would be ready for occupancy this summer, besides the hotel and boarding houses, but such is the fact. Messrs. Davis & Townshend have opened a store for the benefit of summer residents at the Park. It is under the management of Mr. Charles S. Davis, of the above firm.*

From this update, we can surmise that the Mt. Lake Park Hotel, Allegheny House, Thompson (later the Deaconess) Cottage, Mr. Allen's, and Rev. Masden's and a "large number of cottages" were completed by July 1882. We also know that the tabernacle was under construction in late June because there was a serious accident when some scaffolding fell and three were injured. (More on this in the later chapter "Calamites".)

S. L. Allen's Cottage, now known as "The Gables", ca. 1925. Courtesy of Kathie Smith.

Of course, when a cottage is "completed" is a relative term. There was an element of 'pioneering' during those first few summers, with many visitors in tents, Mrs. John Thompson recalled.[9]

"every drop of water (had) to be carried from the old auditorium grounds, where we had, that first summer, a common well." **Mary Thompson, recalling the summer of 1882.**

By the end of the summer of 1882, the founder's "big idea" of creating a religious summer resort was well on its way to becoming a reality. There would be struggles, but, ultimately, it far exceeded what they expected.

4 - THE IMPORTANCE OF THE RAILROAD

"Mountain Lake Park was founded on Idealism and Mountain Air, <u>and Visitors delivered by Rail.</u>" – quote from Mary Love, amended by this Author.

In the early 1880s, travel by large numbers of people, by road, any distance beyond 10 or 15 miles was just not practical. A carriage, pulled by a walking horse, can travel around 3 miles per hour.[1] By railcar, a person could travel up to 100 miles in under three hours.[2] In the previous chapter we saw that the founders rejected a section of land deemed "too far" from the railroad, and they settled on Hoye's Pasture, which had more than a mile of railroad frontage. Without railroad access, scaling up to a proper summer resort would not have been possible.

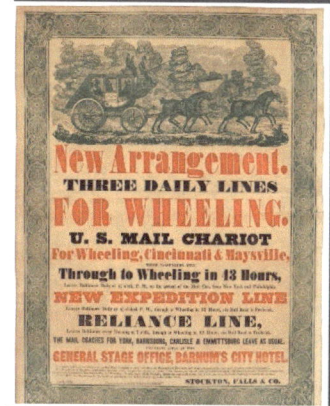

Advert, heralding Baltimore to Wheeling in <u>43 hours</u> via mail coach

Mr. Garrett said he would do all in his power to promote the interests of the association and promised to send Mr. Randolph as soon as possible to act with Col. Woods in locating the depot, lake, etc. **The Republican, Oct. 8, 1881**

The association moved quickly to secure agreements with the B & O, to establish a station at the to-be-formed resort in the fall of 1881. Of course, the B &O agreement was in keeping with the original idea that this would be a rather strict summer resort, so there would be no trains stopping in the Park on Sunday.[3]

The very first groups of people that came to the park, came via rail, on Nov. 1, 1881, and again on May 18, 1882, on "excursion trains", to review the resort location and to bid on building lots.[4]

An early view of the Park train station, said to be taken by a student of the MLP Amateur School of Photography. This is prior to 1895, as the left platform is not enclosed for baggage yet and the 1894 ice house is not visible in the background

21

The Importance of the Railroad

By 1881, the B & O was already heavily invested in the resort business in Garrett County. They owned and operated their own resort hotels in Deer Park and Oakland and these enjoyed strong demand. This new resort would be different than their more stylish, and expensive, resorts; it would cater to a more modest crowd, to those attracted by the religious activities. The B & O would not own the Park resort, but they would work closely with the Association to help ensure its success.

Over the years, the B & O engaged in many projects that provided roads and infrastructure around the Park; they helped to expand and improve the dam, to enlarge the mountain lake, built a side-track to the lake for ice harvesting, graded and built the road towards the "camp ground" (Arbutus Drive, this was before State Route 135) and many other projects.

Railroad Accommodations.

MOUNTAIN LAKE PARK

Is on the Main Line of the B. & O. R. R. The accommodations are first-class, including every comfort that can be furnished by fast vestibule trains, Parlor and Pullman cars. Passengers are landed in the beautiful depot directly at the Park. All trains stop from June 1st to October 31st, save on Sundays.

From the 1896 Mountain Chautauqua

The reason for this collaboration with the Association was simple- the Association needed the railroad to bring the visitors, and the railroad saw opportunities to sell tickets and move freight. In the early 1880s, the B & O entered into an agreement to provide ticket "rebates" to the Association; this agreement specified that the B & O would "rebate" 10% of every ticket sold to-and-from Mt. Lake Park. These rebates were an important source of revenue for the association; in 1891 alone, the association received $1372.00 in rebates.[5]

The alliance reached far beyond rebates and road building.

> The B. & O. R. R. Co. put out 35,000 booklets telling about the Bible Conference and the Chautauqua.

From The Republican, July 23, 1914

The B & O also printed and distributed flyers marketing the events at the Park as well as scheduling heavily discounted "excursion trains" for big events. These excursion trains would offer discounted fares, and dedicated routes to Mt. Lake. The B & O even utilized a dedicated "excursion agent" to schedule and market the excursions to Mt. Lake Park.[6]

> Three Express Trains each way daily. Parlor and Sleeping Cars. Three Mails each way daily. New York and Philadelphia Papers received on day of issue. Season Excursion Tickets at moderate rates. Special Excursion Tickets to Assemblies, Excursions, &c.
> ☞ OVER FIVE THOUSAND PEOPLE visited Mountain Lake Park during its Fifth Season—the Summer of 1886.

From an 1887 Advertisement

B&O Station looking West, before 1907. Loch Lynn and Rathburn Planing Mill on Left (small Mill office in front of Mill building) **Photo taken from the telegraph tower. Courtesy of B & O Railroad Museum, Baltimore, Md.**

In the spring of 1882, the association granted a 3 year lease to Mr. A.R. Sperry. Mr. Sperry built a small (18 x 20 feet) depot building, with a store, later that summer and assumed the job of Railroad agent at the Park[7]. In 1883, the Association granted one acre of land to the B&O, stipulating that they build a train depot, and that no trains would stop at the Park on Sundays[8]. The B&O agreed; a station was built in 1884, and trains did not stop on Sunday in Mt. Lake Park until well after 1910[9]. Because Mt. Lake was a summer resort, the trains only stopped at the Park from June 1st through the end of October.[10]

The Importance of the Railroad

Waiting for Excursion Train to Mountain Lake Park, from Williams, WV. Courtesy West Virginia and Regional History Center, West Virginia University Libraries

SOURCE: Historic photograph "Inside the B&O Passenger Car" J. G. Farrell Railroad Collection; Garrett County History-Homepage (http//www.marylandfamilies.com/).

Looking East, West bound Train Arriving
Courtesy B&O Railroad Museum, Baltimore

Another important feature of the railroad station was the telegraph office. This enabled near-instant communication both East and West of the Park. The 1st mention of a plan for the telegraph office, to be in the initial depot in Mt. Lake, is on March 23, 1882.[11] One of the later telegraph operators, after 1900, was Mr. Edwin O. Fouch, who owned a house on "N" street.

The B&O also enabled newspapers from New York and Washington to be delivered, "same day".[12]

MLP B&O Station with Telegraph Office Sign – Late 1890s.

24

The Importance of the Railroad

Another view of the B&O Station, Post Office & Store in Background on Left. Prior to 1907

During the Park's (and the railroad's) heyday, around 1902, there were more than 40,000 passengers coming and going during a single summer season.[13] B&O Agent H.M. Weeks recalled arriving Park excursion trains that were often 12 coaches long, with between one and two thousand people on board.[14] Return ticket sales could total more than $3000 in one summer day.

Once a visitor arrived at the Depot, there were baggage handlers, hack drivers, and a boardwalk to the resort, as well as a small store and post office right next door.

H.M. Weeks in later years. Courtesy Glade Star, Vol. 4 No.9 1971

Station Force 1913, Hubert M. Weeks, Agent, John McIntosh, Clerk, John Martin, Baggage Handler   Note the baby carriage on top. Mr. Weeks was the B&O Agent from 1913 until 1952. Courtesy Kevin Callis.

25

H.M Weeks, John McIntosh, 1913. Courtesy of Garrett County Historical Society

One of the signs from the Train Depot, now hanging in Town Hall.

With the rise of the automobile, the passenger trains to the Park began their inevitable demise. As people stopped riding the trains, they also ceased coming to Mt. Lake Park. This was not the only reason for the Park's decline, but it was a major contributor. This topic is explored in more detail at the end of this book. Agent H.M. Weeks worked at Mt. Lake nearly 40 years, until 1952. The train station closed for good in 1956.

We think of this pic as the "Last Train."

Right, Interior of the Depot today, supports for pavilion still intact; it is used for commercial business, including this salon.
Photo Courtesy of Jennifer Paugh

5 - THE POST OFFICE, BOARDWALK, AND PILGRIMS' REST

"This place surely is a Pilgrim's Rest!" Rev. John Thompson, 1882.

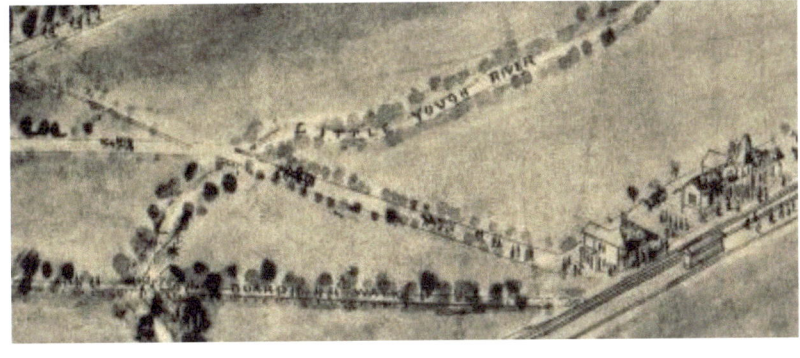

The post office was an important element of the Park, as this enabled near continuous postcard, telegraph, and mail communication with the folks back home. There were 3 mail trains, each way, on every day except Sunday (of course). The first postmaster of the Park was Abram Rhodes Sperry[1].

A post office was built right next to the B&O depot, and alongside the railroad tracks and also housed a general merchandise store, Martin & King, in the same building.

Post Office, Prior to 1908

The Post Office, Boardwalk, & Pilgrims' Rest

MOUNTAIN LAKE PARK SUFFERS LOSS BY FIRE

New Association Building Used for Postoffice and Store Destroyed.

LOSS WILL AGGREGATE $8,000

Postmaster Rudisill Saved His Records By Having Them at His Home—Martin & King, Loose Heaviest—Building Insured for $2500.

Monday night the most destructive fire ever visiting Mountain Lake Park occurred when the new Association building erected last spring at a cost of more than $4000, was destroyed with all its contents, including the stock of merchandise owned by Messrs. Martin & King, general merchants, and the post office.

The post office in the picture, above, built in 1906, was destroyed by fire on November 5, 1907. This was headline news in the Republican Paper on Nov. 7, 1907. The fire was of suspicious origin, and not the only one around this timeframe. This fire dealt a serious financial blow to one of the investors in the store. (See the Calmities chapter for more on that.)

> The fire was discovered shortly after midnight, indications pointing to the fact that it had its inception in the basement of the building, where less than a month ago a fire was discovered in a lot of litter but was put out before much damage was done to the building. At the time the fire was discovered Tuesday morning it had made such headway as to make it impossible to save the building and the energies of the people assembled were turned towards saving the merchandise of Messrs. Martin & King, but comparatively little was gotten out.

NEW BUILDING WILL BE ERECTED

To Take Place of the Postoffice Structure at Mountain Lake Park.

At the special meeting of the directors of Mountain Lake Park Association, held in Baltimore yesterday, a contract was awarded Mr. M. M. Schrock for the erection of a new post-office building at Mountain Lake Park to replace the building destroyed by fire several years ago, work upon which is to begin at an early day.

After the 1907 Post Office fire, it was nearly four years before a new post office building was built, this one in the same general location but set back from the railroad tracks, and a couple hundred yards to the west. The mail was handled out of a building in Loch Lynn Heights during the interim. A May 25, 1911 report in the Republican indicates the contract to build was awarded to Mr. M.M Schrock., builder and owner of several Park cottages.

Post office on the right, after 1911. Depot, Left center. Looking Southeast, on Arbutus Dr. Loch Lynn Peoples store in Background, center.
Courtesy of Bob Boal

28

The Post Office, Boardwalk, & Pilgrims' Rest

Post Office after 1911, looking Northwest. To the left is the start of the boardwalk, and to the right is Arbutus Drive, the road leading into the Park.. (Prior to State. Route 135) Sign on the pole says "Loch Lynn Garage".
Courtesy of Martha Kahl

Walking up the Boardwalk towards the Park, the first structure a visitor would encounter was "Pilgrim's Rest".

Passing through Pilgrim's Rest, heading towards the Park. Post Card courtesy of Bob Boal

Pilgrim's Rest served as a resting place for the rather long walk from the Park to the Depot and Post office. Visitors would usually make at least one trip a day to the post office, to check the mail or pick up a newspaper. Pilgrims' Rest provided a social spot, out of the weather, for exchanging the news of the day and visiting with friends.

The origin of the naming of "Pilgrims' Rest" is provided by the late Jered W. Young; some interviews credit Rev. D.B. Updegraff with the naming of Pilgrims' Rest.[2] Other accounts specifically credit the "Bishop" John Thompson for naming the spot. From reading the description of the Park at that time, this story would take place in June of 1882:

"When the train stopped at Mt. Lake Park, there was no station platform and the good Bishop slipped in the mud and rolled to the bottom of the bank. He finally picked himself up, and he and his followers began to walk to their 'Tent City,' as it was then called.

"Their encampment and the unfinished tabernacle lay on the distant hillside, across the roadless pasture and an unbridged stream. They struck across the glades, along the banks of the Little Yough river, and finally found a place where some herdsmen had erected a rough log shelter.

"Here, worn and weary, they rested, and joined in prayer. After the concluding 'amen,' one of the group exclaimed, 'This place surely is a pilgrim's rest!' A few years later, a wide board walk was built from the post office to the tabernacle, and on this spot was built a small structure with a roof, and benches to sit on. The spot was known thereafter as 'Pilgrim's Rest'."

Boardwalk and Pilgrim's Rest, after 1911. Looking towards Post Office, in left background, rail cars on right.

The Post Office, Boardwalk, & Pilgrims' Rest

E.R. Davis Sr. Aug 18, 1901. Rare Photo taken inside Pilgrim's Rest
Mr. Davis and family rented the Altamont Cottage for more than 20 summers.
Courtesy J.Horner Davis IV

Pilgrims' Rest from Little Yough, downstream. Note the youth on the bridge.

Photo Courtesy of Martha Kahl

Colorized Postcard of the Boardwalk. The "state of the art" sidewalk of the day.
Early on, a boardwalk was constructed; it served a very practical purpose. Otherwise, everyone would be slipping and sliding through the mud.

The Boardwalk was damaged by floods several times over the years, usually when the dam at the Mt. Lake gave way. Here is one account of a 1896 flood, the article is found in the 7/16/1896 edition of the Republican paper:

> *In the meantime, the Little Yough had but raised very much but the great pressure of water back of the dam at Mountain Lake Park eventually broke a hole in the embankment fifty feet wide and the flood came tearing through, dislodging bridges and flooding the glades to a depth of several feet. The water also washed the platform away leading from the Park to the depot at Mt. Lake.*

Mr. A. E. Rambeau remembered another flood and another encounter with water in 1898.[3] Mr. Rambeau's father taught language courses at the Mt. Chautauqua summer schools

The dam at the lake gave way in 1898. It rained nearly all summer of that year. Harry "Buck" Armstrong, Gay Armstrong and Howard Swan and myself made a raft out of the boardwalk during this flood. We had a great time. I also remember a water trough (other than the one in front of the Association cottage), for three of us fell in after imbibing too much blackberrywine.

Boardwalk after a flood, ca 1898. Prior to 1918 because the Loch Lynn Hotel can be seen in the background. Photo From the E.W. Shirer Collection

As nearly as we can determine, the Boardwalk was torn up in the 1950s. Both Mayors Don Sincell (Mt. Lake) and Carolyn Corley (Loch Lynn) remember that Pilgrims' Rest was still standing around 1960.

6 - GETTING ABOUT, HORSES, HACKS & LOCAL EXCURSIONS

'Hack up in the Park! Hack up in the Park- anyplace you want to go!' – Jack Echard

Another option for getting around, once a visitor arrived in Mt. Lake, was to either get a ride with a Hack (the "Uber" of that era) or to rent your own cart or carriage.

Leona Hardesty wrote about the Park and the Dawson family recollections in the Sept. 1969 edition of the Glade Star: *"Mrs. Dawson related that she could still hear Mr. Jack Echard yelling at the station, 'Hack up in the Park- anyplace you want to go!'. Apparently, business was so flourishing that there was enough patronage for all. Mr. Dawson earned some money driving a three-seated buck board wagon to scenic Swallow Falls for Jack Echard. Mr. Dawson earned a salary of 25 cents!"*

Echard's Livery was located where the 400 block of D Street is today.[1]

There were at least two liveries in Mt. Lake Park and Sebold's Livery in Loch Lynn, with several more in Oakland. Many advertised "safe horses".

Jack McGuffin, a black man, was another one of the drivers during Jack Echard's excursions. It is said he drove an eight-seated spring wagon with four horses.[2] He drove visitors to Swallow Falls, Conneway Tower (Backbone Mtn), and the Boiling Spring near Deer Park.

Hitching Post, Loch Lynn Casino. ca. 1900

Getting About; Horses, Hacks & Local Excursions

This appears as if it could be the same pony in two different pictures, pulling two different carts. The picture on the right is E.R. Davis, Sr. with J.Horner Davis II and possibly E.R. Davis, Jr., in the Park, around 1901. Not much is known about the photo on the left., from a Mt. Lake Park collection. Note that "Blair Photography" can be seen in the background.

Courtesy J.Horner Davis IV ca. 1901

Rates Per Passenger.

MILES.		
7	Boiling Spring,	$ .75
5	Deer Park,	.50
3	Oakland and Monte Vista,	.50
1½	Oakland, Round Trip,	.25
8	Deer Park and Treusdale Farm,	.75
6	Allegheny Heights,	.75
6	Hooppole Drive,	.75
10	Lake Brown,	1.00
9	Eagle Rock,	1.00
10	Swallow Falls,	1.00
9	Table Rock, Mt. View Tower,	1.00
14	McHenry Springs, Delawder's,	1.25
14	Brookside and Aurora,	1.00
8¼	North Glade Fishing Club,	1.00

NOT LESS THAN 5 PASSENGERS AT THESE RATES.

Two Seated Carriage, half day,	$3 to 4
" " " per day,	4 to 6
Three " " " hour,	1.50
" " " half day,	3 to 4
" " " per day,	5 to 6
Horse and Buggy, per hour,	$1.00
" " " half day,	2.00
" " " per day,	3.00
One Horse Rubber Tire Runabout per day,	$4.00
" " " " half day,	2.50

Rates to be Posted.

The Mountain Lake Park Community has passed a law that the transfer wagons shall post in their hacks the standard rates of trensfer about the local points and between the Park and Oakland. The step was opposed by some hackmen but the Community insisted that it was proper that there should be similar rate for both stranger and those who know the prices by living here. Complaints had been made of over charges on the part of some hackmen.

The Republican July 11, 1907.

Hack Fare Card after 1907

After 1907, it became a bit more straight-forward to hire a hack, because the hackman were required to post their standard rates. There was concern that "strangers" were being charged more than "locals".

Note the ride is more expensive if the carriage has rubber tires.

From reviewing the fare card, we can get a good sense of the popular "day trip" destinations. Swallow Falls, and McHenry Springs were popular even back then, as were several spots near the Deer Park Hotel, such as the Boiling Spring and the Truesdale Farm (known for its high mountain views.). From the card, it would cost five people $5.00 to go to Swallow Falls. The trip could take over three hours each way. From the recollection of Mr. Dawson earlier, the driver would get 25 cents.

Another approach, popular with groups, was to rent several carriages and drivers and create a "day trip" excursion:

"The Epworth League excursion to Boiling Spring Tuesday afternoon was participated in by about seventy-five Leaguers and others, who were conveyed to that delightful spot by two large hay wagons and other vehicles. A bountiful lunch was spread in the evening of which all partook heartily except Albert White —who said he hadn't seen so much good eatin's for a long time, and were it not for a case of dyspepsia he would have enjoyed the lunch immensely. The party returned home before dark."[3]

Day Trip Excursion in Garrett County. Courtesy of Sarah Steyer.

TUESDAY, AUG. 19.
EXCURSION DAY.—Points of interest: "Deer Park," "Boiling Spring," "Eagle Rock," "Oakland," "Big Yough," "Buckhorn Wall," etc.

Not all the excursions went according to plan. Here is a story captured in the Republican paper on May 24, 1896, titled, "Lost!" The driver in the story is James O. Smith, "Miss Jenny" Smith's brother, who was an active wagon driver in the Park. Also mentioned in the story is a one of the chaperones, Mrs. Hayden. This would presumably be James Hayden's wife, Lititia; Capt. Hayden was the founder of the Republican newspaper, among other achievements.

> ### Lost!
> On Wednesday of last week, a party of ladies and gentlemen started from the Park on a pleasure trip. Madames Hayden and Hocking were chosen as chaperones. They selected a point near Swallow Falls for their picnic grounds. There were several of the party who knew just where Swallow Falls was located, notably the two chaperones. Oh, yes! they knew all about it; could not be mistaken in the route. So did Capt. James Smith, the driver of the conveyance which contained this precious load of merry makers. They passed through Oakland about 9 a. m.; as the wheels went rolling along the road toward their destination, they were too happy to think of anything but themselves. Presently one more considerate of their future happiness than the others asked Mr. Smith if the road did not look a little unfamiliar to him. Mr. S., looking dazed, acknowledged that the road did look a little strange.
> Thereupon a doubt arose in the minds of the entire party. "Oh! dear, what shall we do," several exclaimed in concert. "Surely we are on the wrong road." At this point a wayfaring man hove in sight. As he drew near Mr, Smith asked him, "Where are we?" "You are right here by that big stump," replied the man. "Can you tell us how far it is to Swallow Falls," asked one of the excited chaperones. "Yes, madam, go back about two miles, then turn to your right and go two miles more and you will see the falls. Why not continue on your journey; it is but a short distance to Muddy Falls, and a delightful place it is, too."
> "Muddy Falls! Muddy Falls! Oh! let us go to Muddy Falls!" they cried, as if by inspiration they had been impressed with the beauty and grandeur of this haven of rest.
> "Why, ladies, understood you when you left the Park, that I was to drive to Muddy Falls," said the wily Capt. Smith. In due time they arrived at Lake Lewis, where their hunger was appeased by a bountiful supply of the necessaries of life. After dinner and lunch at Hotel Saw Mill this happy party returned home at about 10 p. m., singing, "Home Again, Home Again."

SWALLOW FALLS, MOUNTAIN LAKE CHAUTAUQUA.

These excursions and picnics, while pleasant, were not the main force pulling visitors to the Park. It started with the religious camp meetings, quickly followed by the summer schools and capped by the Chautauqua performers. Now that we have a glimpse of how people got around, we turn our attention to the "main events".

From The Chautauquan Magazine Vol 31 1900

7 - THE CAMP MEETINGS, SUMMER SCHOOLS AND CHAUTAUQUA ASSEMBLIES.

The history of the Mountain Chautauqua at Mt. Lake, though it started a few years later, closely tracks the evolution of the Chautauqua movement in the United States. What started in 1873 at Lake Chautauqua in upstate New York as religious and educational events centered on "Camp Meetings", quickly grew to add "Summer Schools", at first to train Sunday School teachers, and later expanding to liberal and fine arts education.[1] And as the Chautauqua movement grew, the assembly included an increasing number of "acts" that served a heavy dose of entertainment as well as education.

The summertime Chautauqua Assemblies spread far and wide. By 1905, there were over 233 "Daughter Chautauqua's" in more than 32 States, in addition to Indian Territory (now Oklahoma) and Canada.[2] All these Chautauquas created a strong demand for lecturers and entertainers, enabling a kind of "circuit" where performers would travel from Chautauqua to Chautauqua. In Mt. Lake, from 1890 to 1912, W.L. Davidson was largely responsible for organizing the summer program, and he spent a great deal of time traveling to "book the talent".

W. L. Davidson, D. D.
Lexington, Ky., and Mountain Lake Park, Md.

From The Chautauqua Magazine Vol 16 1892-1893

Another component of the Chautauqua experience was the Chautauqua Literary Scientific Circle or C.L.S.C. These study groups developed at nearly every Chautauqua location and were organizations to provide a study circle for a specific curriculum of religious, philosophical, and scientific literature. Each year, the Park's C.L.S.C. members would hold a formal graduation ceremony for students that completed studies; this was called "recognition day" and it was often one of the biggest events of the season. After the Hall of Philosophy was built, the faculty, students, graduates, lecturers, and flower girls would assemble there, then march to the tabernacle, the graduates crossing through an archway to receive their "seals" (diplomas) on the platform. This ceremony closely tracked the same proceeding in Chautauqua, New York.[3]

In 1905, Mt. Lake Park was identified as one of the top five Chautauqua's in the country, with a full bill of camp meetings, more than 25 summer school "departments", and the best entertainment available on the Chautauqua circuit.[4]

In the Park, the first camp meetings were held in 1882, and the initial summer schools were organized in 1884, when an already-formed C.L.S.C. from Harrisburg, Pa. decided to relocate their summer studies to the park.[5] At first, just a handful of summer classes were offered, but more education was added each summer, until, after 1900, up to 25 departments taught classes on everything from Greek, Elocution, Photography, Mathematics, Wood Carving, Bookkeeping, Astronomy, Kindergarten Training, Cooking, and anything in between. Tracing the evolution of the Chautauqua assembly, we will provide details on the Park's Camp Meetings, Summer Schools, and, finally, the entertainments in the following sections.

Camp Meetings: Some Movers and Shakers

"...if anyone made any "slips" this year, I know of no better repair shop than the Mt. Lake Park Camp Meeting." **Rev. John Thompson, 1896, in the Hall of Philosophy.**[1]

Camp Meetings were the driving force for the creation of the summer Park. These summer events were a key element to rural life in West Virginia, Western Maryland and Pennsylvania. Many of the Park Camp Meetings were associated with the holiness movement and were highly-charged, emotional affairs.[2] While the services and attendees tilted strongly in the direction of Methodists, several other religious organizations and denominations, such as Quakers and Holiness Pentecostals, were also welcomed to the Park. These organizations held conferences and camp meetings that drew in thousands of visitors.

"I was here four years ago, and I received such an uplift that I have not got over it yet." **Rev. Ruth, 1896.**[3]

Camp Meeting at Assembly Hall & Tabernacle, Superintendent's office in background. July 15, 1907. Courtesy of Sarah Steyer.

The camp meetings generally ran during the early part of the season, in July, followed by the Chautauqua performers in August. The summer schools bridged both these events, as did the numerous conferences of groups such as the Epworth League and the Independent Order of Odd Fellows.

Some Profiles

As the Park was founded as a Methodist-oriented religious resort, there were far too many preachers and evangelists that passed through the place than we have pages; we will try to highlight the most influential and dramatic "movers and shakers" here.

Miss Jennie Smith and Adelaide "Addie" Sherman

"What a strange place for a camp meeting, in this wilderness! I wonder if our feet will ever tread that ground?"
Jennie Smith, passing by Mt. Lake Park via Rail on May 13, 1882.[4]

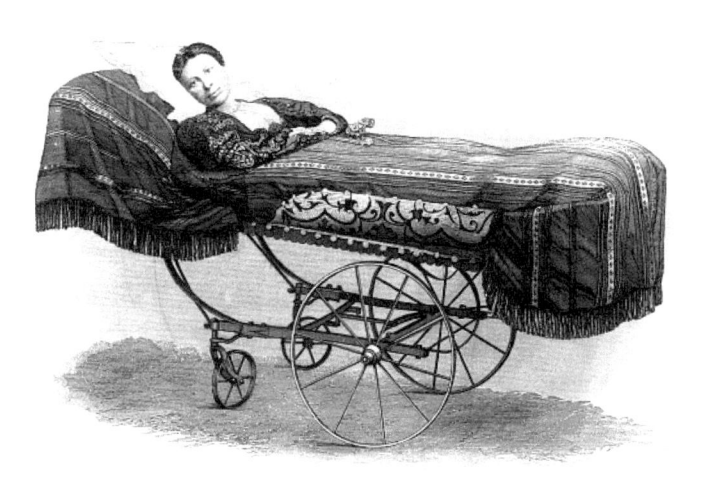

Perhaps no other evangelist personifies the Mt. Lake Park religious spirit than "Miss Jennie" Smith. Her story is one of dramatic illness and then of a "miraculous cure". Along the way, she found religion, set out on an odyssey of "saving" folks, raising money, building a hotel in Mt. Lake and endlessly preaching.

Miss Smith was struck down with a spinal illness at the age of 15; she subsequently traveled to several parts of the U.S.

Miss Jennie in her Mobile "Railroad Bed"

seeking treatment. She traveled in a specially designed bed, which enabled her to travel by train.

On the trains, she had to travel in the baggage car and she spent a great deal of time with the railroad workers there. She eventually recovered from her illness at the age of 31.[5] The railroad workers became appreciative of her condition and recovery and ultimately raised monies for her, with no one worker allowed to contribute more than $1 per person, so that she might be able to buy a home. In 1883-1884, with this money and other money that she raised, she ended up building the "Grace Cottage" (really a hotel) in the Park. (Grace Cottage later became Chautauqua Hotel.)[6]

Jennie Smith after recovery

In, 1883, Miss Jennie's extended family also relocated to Mt. Lake. Her sisters, brothers, their spouses, and others played an important role in the lodging trade in the Park.

Miss Jennie got a job as the "Railroad Evangelist" for the Women's Christian Temperance Union (W.C.T.U). This job took her far and wide, and gave her endless opportunities to preach and attempt to convert people. To get a sense of the level of her travels and activities, we need only look at one annual report she submitted to the W.C.T.U:

> Miss Jennie Smith has labored with her usual faithfulness and success the past year, averaging, as will be seen by the brief statistical report furnished and appended, much over one public meeting each day. During the coming year state superintendents are urged to systematize as much as possible the work of "Sister Jennie," so as to avoid unnecessary expense and travel, and to urge the local unions to so arrange that financial support may more adequately meet the needs of this valuable worker and dear sister. Her labors should be supplemented by an accredited railway evangelist in each state.
>
> REPORT OF EVANGELIST.
>
> Public meetings addressed, besides fourteen all day meetings........352
> Railroad shop meetings held....................................41
> Citizens' firemen   "   " 10
> Police court   "   " 8
>
> One thousand four hundred Railroad Temperance Association buttons given out and pledge cards.
> Seven thousand railroad greetings given out.
> Four thousand printed cards.
> One thousand three hundred tracts and papers.
> Sixty calenders and scrap books.
> About five hundred conversions.
> Several hundred families visited and prayed with.
> I have spent more in hotels, railroad fare and other expenses than I have received during the year.
>
> JENNIE SMITH.
> *Railroad Evangelist.*

She reports that she spent more money than she received during the year, participated in at least 352 meetings and effected "about 500" conversions, all in a single year.

When she was not riding the rails, Miss Jennie was very active in preaching in Mt. Lake Park and the surrounding areas. Although she was warmly regarded, she ofttimes appeared to be at odds with the MLP association board, and the issues were usually about money.[7] She wrote four books; each based upon different phases of her life story, including "Incidents and Experiences of a Railroad Evangelist". In this book, Jennie writes of her struggles with her health and with money; the following excerpt describes a time when she fell ill and lost Grace Cottage (also later called Thorburn Inn):

> For many weeks I was unconscious; they said my flesh looked like varnished mahogany. During this time my mortgage came due. Others lifted it, which gave them charge of the place. They changed the name from "Grace" to *"Chautauqua Hotel."*
>
> I could not meet the demands, so in the course of time I lost everything. Had any one told me I could give up my home and all I loved so dearly with such peace of mind and resignation, I could not have believed it. After a little struggle I had the victory; grace was sufficient.

Camp Meetings, Summer Schools, & Chautauqua Assemblies

After losing the hotel, Miss Jennie said she felt freed from her material obligations and able to concentrate on her preaching. She continued to travel for the W.T.C.U. and preached far and wide, often coming back to the Park. She wrote her last book, the Incidents and Experiences, etc., in 1920. Jennie Smith died in 1924.

Addie Sherman was a co-worker with Miss Jennie, also a railroad evangelist. Although her story was not as dramatic as Miss Jennie's, she spent many years traveling and preaching with the W.C.T.U. When not traveling, she lived in Mt. Lake, for some seasons at the Grace Cottage. When Addie Sherman died on June 30, 1894, she was buried in the Oakland Cemetery.[8]

The following is an excerpt from Jennie Smith's aforementioned book, describing her last work with Addie Sherman:

MY LAST WORK WITH MISS SHERMAN

was at Ludlow, Louisville, Frankfort, and Covington, Ky., with several services here and there. As she was not well, I left her with our friends, Mr. and Mrs. McLaughlin, in Covington, and returned home. In ten days they brought her; she was partially paralyzed and almost unconscious. She lingered in a stupor for nearly six weeks, only a momentary consciousness now and then. She quietly fell asleep in Jesus and went to her reward. I remained with her during this time.

The funeral was most impressive, was almost like an experience meeting. The pallbearers were all railroad men whom she had led to Christ. They and others testified to what she had done for them. Judge McLaughlin and wife came from Covington, Ky. For fourteen years we labored together, going from the Atlantic to the Pacific, from the lakes to the Gulf. I have never found her equal in

PERSONAL SOUL-WINNING.

Excerpt From Jennie Smith Book

Addie Sherman's estate amounted to more than $10,000 in cash, equivalent to more than $345,000 in 2022 money.⁹ Her will left nearly all the money to the "Woman's Foreign Mission" but because there were two organizations that could claim to be the "Woman's Foreign Mission", the estate was tied up for years, with each group contesting the will.

Addie Sherman and Miss Jennie Smith are buried side by side in the Oakland Cemetery.

Marker photo retrieved from findagrave.com
Note that the year of Adelaide's death does not match newspaper accounts (1894).

Rev. John Thompson

Rev. John Thompson was born in 1823, in Delaware County, Pennsylvania, and although informally educated, he grew up to be a teacher in the public schools there. Shortly afterward Mr. Thompson converted to Methodism and later became a Minister in the Philadelphia Methodist conference.[10]

In mid-life, Rev Thompson was impacted by some sort of debilitating illness. When he was 47 years old, "As a result of excessive labors, he broke down in 1870, and for five years he never read a book or a chapter of the bible."[11]

Mr. Thompson evidently recovered to a large extent because he later became quite active in Mt. Lake Park. He was also the associate editor of the Philadelphia-based Christian Standard Weekly; the July, 1896 edition contains a wide-ranging account of the Pentecostal Services at the Park. "Brother Thompson" figures prominently in this edition, written by Mrs. E.E. Williams.

From the detailed accounts in this one booklet, we can get a good sense of the fervent prayer meetings, with much shouting and exultations. Presiding over these meetings was "Bishop Thompson". Here is a brief excerpt describing a prayer meeting on July 4, 1896 at 7:30pm:

Rev. John Thompson, 1896
Christian Standard

> *Dr. Wm. Spencer, the preacher of the hour, asked Dr. Gilmour to sing,*
> *"In that city, bright city"*
> *The hymn was sung over and over. Reminders were delivered by Dr. Spencer in his own burning fervid style, until the people all over the place were weeping and praising the Lord. Seldom have we witnessed such a scene as this. The people stood, singing, shouting, and waving handkerchiefs, while Dr. Spencer, now praising, now exhorting, swept up and down the platform like one, indeed, on fire of the Holy Ghost! By the time he announced his text, "Let him that heareth say, Come" everything was at white heat of holy fervor, and all minds receptive to the truth.*

Rev. Thompson is also credited with naming the rest area along the boardwalk "Pilgrims' Rest". This story is recounted elsewhere in this book, in the Chapter covering Pilgrims' Rest.

Early on, in 1882, Rev. Thompson built the large "cottage" that would later become the Thompson Rest Home for Deaconesses. This property still stands today. In 1899, as Rev. Thompson was in ill health and losing his eyesight, he and his wife sold their cottage to the Woman's Home Missionary Society and they converted it to the Summer Rest Home for Deaconesses and Missionaries.[12]

Rev. Thompson died on August 3, 1899 at his home in Mt. Lake Park. His wife, Asenath Mary Thompson, was also quite active in the Park. She died in Ohio, in 1916. For some early recollections from Mrs. Thompson, see the write up on the Thompson Rest Home in the chapter on Boarding houses.

Amanda Smith

In the late 1800s, Mrs. Amanda Berry Smith was a well-known Methodist holiness evangelist, traveling missionary, and author. Amanda was born into slavery in 1837, in Long Green, Maryland. After she obtained freedom, she found her calling as a preacher; she traveled extensively and over the course of her travels, she visited Oakland, Deer Park, and Mt. Lake Park several times. In the 1890s and early 1900s, she visited the area and helped to raise money for the A.M.E. church, which was subsequently built in Oakland, Md.

In the summer of 1896, Amanda spoke at the Mt. Lake Camp Meeting.[13] Mrs. E.E. Williams describes the scene of July 5th:

From her 1893 Autobiography.

The people came out in throngs for the love feast, at 9:30am. Sister Amanda Smith was in charge (of the opening of the meeting) …she sang: "Blessed Assurance" ….and said "the Lord is to me this morning more than tongue can tell.….When I think of the privilege I have of being here, and telling you his goodness and mercy, my heart almost breaks with gratitude. I want to shout Hallelujah, because I am saved and kept by the power of God." now she sang, as only Amanda Smith can sing, "My life flows on in an endless song."

Amanda published an autobiography in 1893, titled: <u>An Autobiography, The Story of the Lord's Dealing with Mrs. Amanda Smith, the Colored Evangelist Containing an Account of her Life Work of Faith, and Her Travels in America, England, Ireland, Scotland, India, and Africa, as An Independent Missionary.</u>

One of the more dramatic sections in this book is when Amanda Smith describes buying her sister, Frances, out of slavery; although she was born free in Pennsylvania, her sister had ended up enslaved to a "Mr. Hutchinson" near Monkton, Maryland. The following events took place in 1862, where, in a "border state" such as Maryland, enslavement was still legally practiced:

I don't know how many black people Mr. Hutchinson owned; he was excited over the war; and while he was considered to be a very good man to his black people, yet he was rough when I told him what my errand was. When I told him my sister was freeborn, was not a slave and never had been, he simply said he had nothing to do with that; he had paid forty dollars for her, and he was not going to let her go for less. Well, I didn't know what to do. I cried, but he raved; he swore, and said Frances had not been of any use anyhow. At first he said he would not let her go at all. Then he went into the house. His wife was a very nice woman. How well I remember her. I cried, and cried, and could not stop. I was foolish, but I could not help it. She said something to him. He went into the house, and by and by he came back and said he was not going to let her go for less than forty dollars. Then my sister told me if I would go over to Mrs. Hutchinson's father's (I think his name was Matthews, and he was a Quaker), and see him, she thought he might help me. They were very nice people, and had always been kind to her. It was about a quarter of a mile across the fields. So I went over then and old Mr. Matthews told me I was to go on back, and next morning he would ride over. So, sure enough; next morning the old man came over. He pitied me, I saw, but he could not help me much. Mr. Hutchinson walked up and down and swore. I told Mr. Matthews that I had no money scarcely, and I did not know how to get back if I paid out the forty dollars. I would only have enough to get back to York, and how was I going to get from York to Lancaster, where I lived, and get my sister there besides? Well, Mr. Hutchinson said, he had nothing to do with that. So he told my sister she could get ready and go. I paid him the money. Then she got ready. She went to get her shawl, and he said to her she should not have anything but what she had on. They had given her a shawl, a dress and a pair of great big brogan shoes; and they let her take the dress (a blue cotton striped) she had on; madame had given her a gingham apron; that she was to leave. So we started; just what she stood up in, with one domestic dress under her arm, was all she had. He flourished the horse-whip around so I didn't know but we were both going to get a flogging before we left; but we got out without the flogging. But oh! wasn't he mad! I thanked the Lord for the old Quaker gentleman. But for him it would have been much worse. Then how I prayed the Lord would bless Mrs. Hutchinson. I believe she was good. There were a number of little black children around there, and Mr. Hutchinson was kind to them, and played with them, and put them on the horse and held them on to ride, and they seemed to be very fond of him. But then they were slaves. What a difference it made in his feelings toward them. My sister was free. He had not any business with her, and I had no right to pay him any money; and if I had had as much sense then as I have now, I would not have paid him a cent; I would have just waited till he went to bed, and taken the underground railroad plan. But it is all over now, and my poor sister has long since gone to her reward.

In the late 1890s, enslavement was something that many living blacks had personally experienced earlier in their lives. By 1899, 21 percent of the national black population had been born into slavery, according to historian Mary Frances Berry.

Amana Smith continued to travel and preach well into the 20th century. She also founded an orphanage home in Chicago after 1900. Mrs. Amanda Berry Smith died at her home in Sebring Florida, in 1915.[14]

Regarding the next two missionaries, **Ada Lee and Ida Lee**, there can be some confusion. Ada Lee and Ida Lee were both visitors and summer residents of the park, and they both were married to men named "Rev. Lee". They both traveled to India with their respective husbands and performed missionary work. Ada and Ida were two different unrelated people, as were the two Rev. Lee's.

Ada Lee was a missionary and mother of six children, and when she and her husband, Rev. David Lee, returned to the United States, they often visited Mt. Lake Park.[15] They traveled extensively in India and, on September 24, 1899, their family a met terrible tragedy there. They had left their children with their eldest daughter in Darjeeling, India so that they could travel and do missionary work. During their absence a terrible storm blew up, followed by an earthquake. All of their children took shelter in a house, but then there was a landslide and all but one of the Lee children were killed. The Lee's did not lose their faith and they continued to do missionary work in India for more than 20 years. Ada Lee wrote a few books, including, in 1900, "The Darjeeling Disaster", which chronicles the events surrounding the tragedy. Ada Lee died in India in 1948.

MR. AND MRS. D. H. LEE WITH THEIR CHILDREN FOUR YEARS BEFORE.

Ida Lee and the Rev. Joseph Lee fared a little better than the Ada Lee family. Ida (Engle) Lee was born in Grantsville and married Rev. Joseph Lee, a Methodist minister. The Lee's traveled to India and did missionary work as well, but they developed a strong financial interest in Mt. Lake. Ida Lee owned two houses on E street, not far from Cozy Row. She rented out these two cottages and, in 1895, the Lee's also built a large cottage on "M" street, known as the "Lee Cottage", which still stands today. The Lee's daughter, Nell, inherited Lee Cottage and lived in it for many years.[16] Rev Joseph Lee was an ambitious minister; he wrote a "dictionary of the bible", which is said to run over 5000 pages long.[17] The book was published in Morgantown, West Virginia; fragments of the original manuscript are kept in the Mt. Lake Park History Museum.

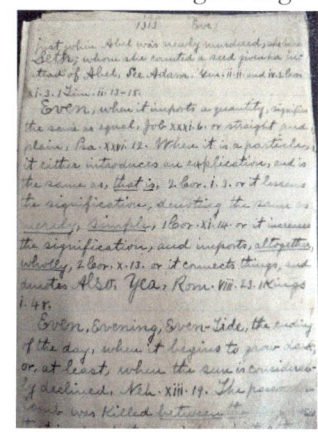

Lee Cottage ca. 1979 Mary Love Collection. Courtesy of Martha Kahl

Page 1313 of Rev. Joseph Lee's Dictionary of the Bible. Courtesy of Jenny & Jim Neville. This page defines the word "Even".

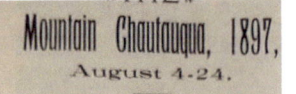

The Summer Schools

The summer schools at the Park were a big draw for visitors from 1883 through 1920.[1] The vacationers that Mt. Lake attracted were interested in leisure, but leisure with a purpose. The summer schools enabled folks to learn new skills and, hopefully, become more enlightened. The specific classes often lasted between two and five weeks, with additional evening lectures as well. The faculty and administrators at Dickinson College in Carlisle, Pennsylvania played a large role in organizing and delivering the classes, with many other people of accomplishment teaching classes as well. This Dickinson College connection was a good fit as it was an early Methodist college and Park leaders, such as John Goucher, Dr. William Frysinger, and Dr. Max Learnd (a dean of the summer schools) were alumni.

The school set up was formal, with a Superintendent and Dean, and many of the teachers were professors or ran their own Institutes in their "day jobs".

These classes were first held at the (old) Auditorium and Mt. Lake Park hotel, and as the park expanded, in the Hall of Philosophy building, and the Bashford Amphitheater.

James H Morgan, one of the Deans of the Summer Schools. Courtesy of Dickinson College Archives

The class subjects ranged from the practical, vocational type subjects such as Stenography and Bookkeeping, (how to teach) Kindergarten, to Language arts, such as German or Greek, right on through Fine Arts, with classes on Painting, Music, and Amateur Photography. In 1892, the tuition for most classes was $3.00 for the entire class.

From the 1884 Mt. Lake Park Messenger The four-year self-study topics of C.L.S.C. were a featured element of many of the classes. The first C.L.S.C. had relocated from Harrisburg, Pa. in 1883, In the early years, one of the many lecturers was Rev J.B. Young, longtime resident Jered Young's father.

The Mt. Lake Park School of Amateur Photography

One of the longest running and best regarded of the summer classes was the School of Amateur Photography. This "School" was founded by Professor Charles F. Himes from Dickinson College and taught by Himes and his assistant, Albert A. Line, also from Carlisle, Pa. From the first summer of the class in 1884, more than 30 students from all over the east coast attended. Many of the Park photos and postcards that we have available today were taken by these photography students and teachers.

Professor Himes

Carlisle Sentinel Aug. 18, 1884. Courtesy of Richard Truitt.

Dr. Himes taught physics at Dickinson; he was highly regarded, giving lectures which demonstrated physics principles in all the major east coast cities. Himes became fascinated with photography and for many years attempted to advance the preservation of documents by taking pictures of them (photo copies). He was ahead of his time in this regard and also in setting up "Photography Exchange" clubs. These exchange clubs could be thought of as an early version of "Instagram". He was certainly a visionary of his time.

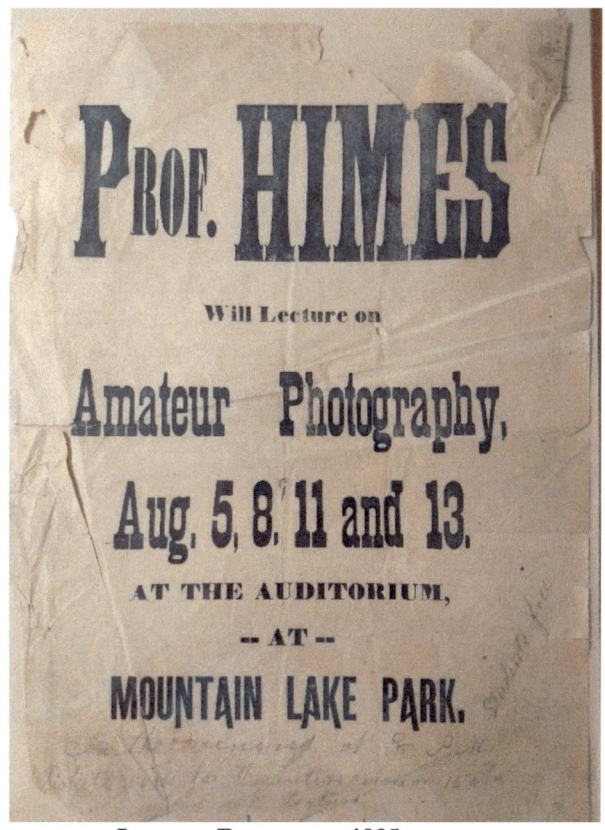

Lecture Poster, ca. 1885
Archives and Special Collections, Dickinson College, Carlisle, PA.

Penciled in on the poster reads, "In the evening at 8pm", "Students free", "50 Cents for the entire course or 15 Cents per lecture".

The school of amateur photography was described as the first of its kind in the country.[2]

MLP Amateur School of Photography ca. 1885 Professor A.A. Line at far right. Also in this group may be "Mrs. Frysinger" and "Miss Van Meter", although we are unable to place them. Taken in the Park "Grove", Superientent's house in the right background.
Courtesy of Cumberland County, Pa. Historical Society

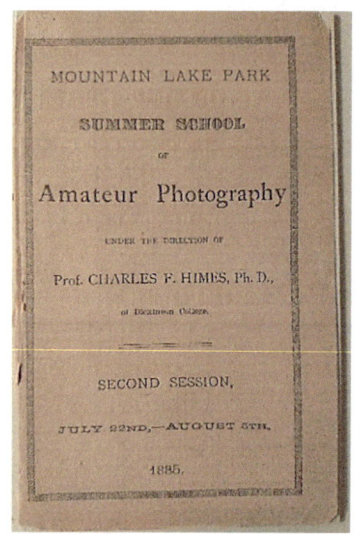

Mt. Lake Park Coursebook 1885
Courtesy Dickinson Archives[3]

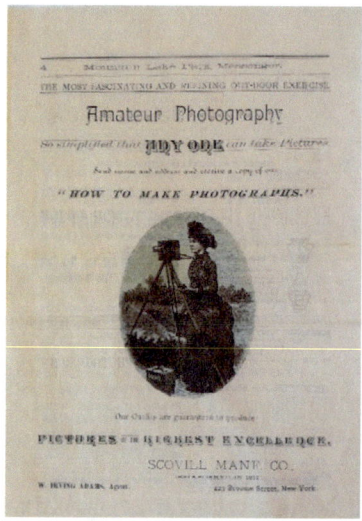

Advertisement MLP Messager 1884

From the advertisement, above, it is apparent that photography was an acceptable pursuit, at least as a hobby, for a young "Lady" in the 1880s. In the photographs we have from the Mt. Lake Park School of Photography, there are many women attending the school.

Professor Himes at work at the Assembly Hall, ca. 1884
Courtesy Dickinson Archives[4]

This Aug. 25, 1884 letter from Albert Line to Professor Himes provides a glimpse of success of the inaugural Photography class.

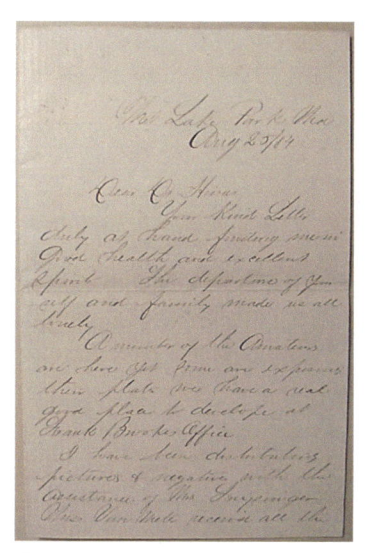

Courtesy Cumberland County Historical Society

Dear Dr. Himes,

Your kind letter in hand, finding me in good health and excellent spirits. The departure of yourself and your family made us all lonely.

A number of Amateurs are here yet; some are exposing their plates. We have a real good place to develop at Frank Brook's office.

I have been distributing pictures and negatives with the assistance of Mrs.(Miss?) Frysinger. Miss Van Meter received all the apparatus and everything seems satisfactory. In fact, the Amateur School of Photography is the marked and leading feature under the auspices of the Park Association this year.

I will remain here until the close of the assembly, returning to Carlisle on Saturday.

With kindest regards to the family, I remain yours

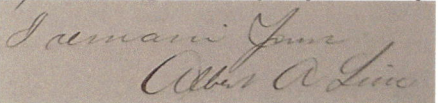

We are always struck by the penmanship and the consise writing when we read these letters.

At the Assembly Hall. Professor Himes right, A.A. Line 2nd from right, Prof. Morgan 2nd from Left.[5]

The students did their part, with pleasurable interest, working early and late, then at night dreaming about their photographs! For hours after the school had finally closed, the room was crowded with persons coming and going, to see and examine the pictures, and great satisfaction was expressed. **Carlisle Sentinel, Aug. 18, 1884.**

Lunch time at the Mt. Lake Summer School. Reverse caption reads "Mt. Lake Park Students, Himes seated, center." ca. 1890 Courtesy Dickinson College Archives[6]

We can imagine that the students and teachers experienced great camaraderie and bonding, especially as the students began to see that they too could produce their own photographs. It likely seemed like magic at the time. The students' excitement is expressed in the following proclamation, in the summer of 1884, at the close of the first summer class.

A Proclamation, Aug. 14, 1884

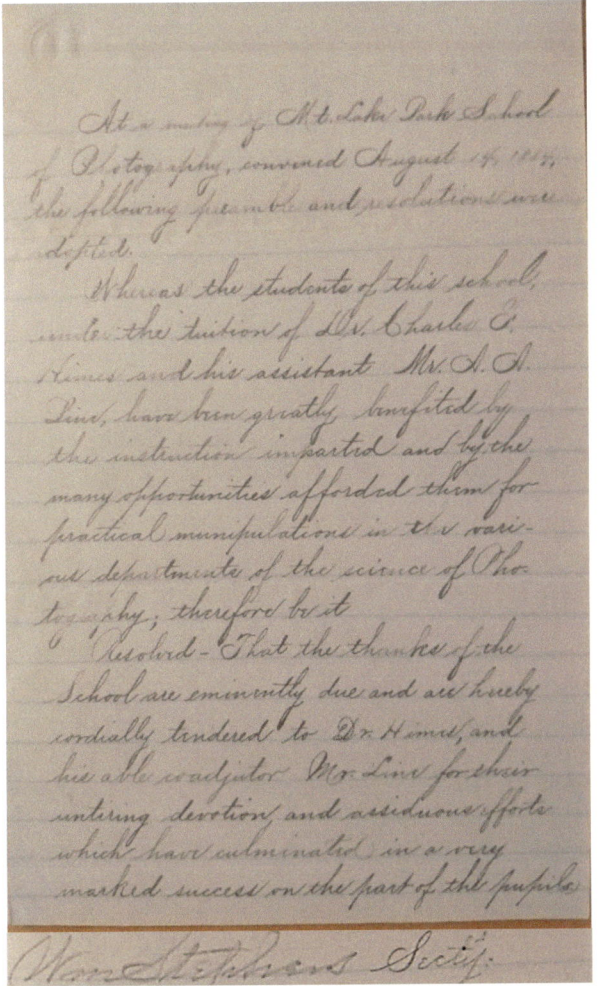

At a meeting of the Mt. Lake Park School of Photography, convened August 14, 1884, the following preamble and resolutions were drafted.

Whereas *the students of this school, under the tuition of Dr. Charles E. Himes and his Assistant, A. A. Line have been greatly benefitted by the instruction imparted and by the many opportunities afforded them by the practical manipulations in the various departments of the science of Photography, therefore be it:*

Resolved *- That the thanks for the school are imminently due and hereby cordially tendered to Dr. Himes, and his coadjutor, Mr. Line, for the untiring devotion and assiduous efforts which have culminated in very marked success on the part of the pupils.*

Resolved *- That we urgently solicit Mt. Lake Park Association to extend to Professor Himes and his assistant an invitation to visit the Park next summer and re-establish his school of Photography, feeling fully assured from the great benefits already derived by the present class, from his instructions, there will be developed, a greater and growing interest, which cannot fail to inure to the Advantage of the Park Association.*

Wm. Stephens, Secty.

Courtesy Cumberland County Historical Society

These classes continued through 1900 and beyond. At some point in the late 1880s, Professor Himes turned the entire class over the Albert Line. Professor Himes was named President of Dickinson College and that may have reduced his availability. There are photos of Mr. Line in this book, a much older man, in Mt. Lake Park after the 1900.

Amateur Photography Class ca. 1885 Assembly Hall and Tabernacle in Background. Albert Line standing, center. Courtesy of Cumberland County, Pa. Historical Society

The Stereopticon was a big innovation in the late 1800s. Albert Line produced and sold these types of stereo views. This particular device is dated 1897. Found in the Carr Cottage. Courtesy of Sarah Haynes.

Around the turn of the Century, the "Brownie" camera was invented[7] and this spelled beginning of the end of complex amateur photography and photo development. It appears that the school of amateur photography ran through the first several years of the 20th century.

Art School

Several different artists and teachers came to teach art classes over the years, including (Emma) Eva Hubbard, Emily Noyes Vanderpoel, Professor W.M.R. French, and Miss Jennie White. We will highlight a few of these teachers below.

Emma Eva Hubbard was an accomplished artist and teacher; she taught art classes at Mt. Lake Park in the late 1880s. Eva was born in Iowa in 1858 and by the age of 18 she had moved to Morgantown, W.Va. and graduated from the Morgantown Female Seminary. She ultimately became the first head of the West Virginia University Department of Art in 1897.

Mt. Lake Park Summer Art School.
The third annual session will begin July 1, 1887. The course of instruction includes Drawing Lessons from casts and objects, Studies from Life Models, Landscape, Flower and Portrait Painting and Crayon Portraits. Special attention given to Studies from Life and Sketching from Nature. For terms and further information address
MRS. EVA HUBBARD,
Mt. Lake Park, Md.

The Republican July, 1887

Eva Hubbard, 1897,
Courtesy West Virginia and Regional History Center, West Virginia University Libraries

Eva's bio is retrieved from WVU's history site:

E. Eva Hubbard was a graduate of Morgantown Female Seminary (1876). Early widowhood led her to pursue a career in art to support her child and mother. Hubbard taught in private studios and at home in Wheeling, Mountain Lake Park, Maryland and Morgantown, and was occasionally affiliated with the Morgantown public schools before accepting the position as instructor and becoming first head of WVU's new Department of Art in 1897.

Her students found positions in the fine arts throughout the state's normal school system and one of them, Blanche Lazzell, became nationally known as a modernist. Lazzell kept in close touch with her mentor throughout her life. Before the 1950's both art and music suffered from being considered service units.

During her career Hubbard disputed the subordination of the fine arts in the curriculum. When she unsuccessfully lobbied the Board of Regents in 1912 not to abolish the department, she noted that she had been underwriting the department with fees collected from occasional students, taught courses to engineers and showed considerable success producing fine artists. "The Department has supplied a need and I feel very deeply the wrong of tearing down the work of fifteen years of upbuilding." She reminded the Regents that the General Federation of Women's Clubs would be meeting in Morgantown in October and their help could be recruited in lobbying for continuance of the Department.

Retrieved from West Virginia History on View, West Virginia and Regional History Center, West Virginia University Libraries

Emma Eva Hubbard. *Fall Scene on the Grafton Road, Monongalia County.* Oil on canvas, 15 x 19 inches, ca. 1930. Private collection.

Landscape painting by Eva Hubbard. A number of Hubbard's paintings survive in private collections. Excerpt from <u>**Early Art and Artists in W.Va.**</u>[8]

Not all students of the schools were "out-of-towners", this notice was found in the Sept. 22, 1888 edition of the Republican newspaper:

Mr. J. Lee McComas, youngest son of D. J. Lee McComas, is quite an artist. After thirteen lessons at the Art School of Mrs. Eva Hubbard, at Mt. Lake Park, the only instruction he ever received, he finished a number of paintings which would do credit to one of greater age and more training. These paintings are on exhibition in the parlor of Dr. McComas where they have been favorably criticized by lovers of art.

Emily Noyes Vanderpoel taught art at the Park summer schools in the early 1890s. During this time she lived in New York City and, in later years, she lived in Litchfield, Connecticut. Mrs. Vanderpoel illustrated books and posters and, in 1903, she wrote an art instruction book titled: <u>Color Problems</u>. The book was highly regarded and was considered the most detailed treatment of examining the combined use of oil paint colors to achieve realistic paintings of natural objects. The book runs over 400 pages and has recently been re-issued.

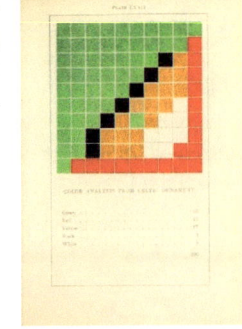

Emily Noyes Vanderpoel in her NYC apt. ca. 1920

<u>**Color Problems**</u> **excerpt, 1903**

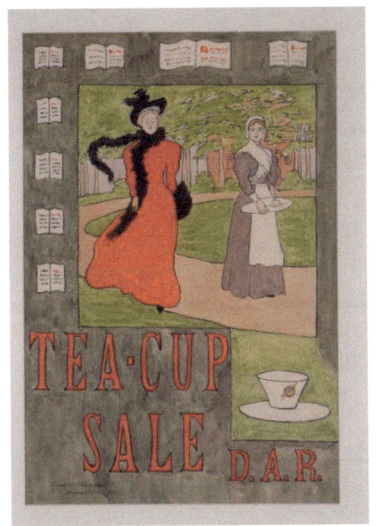

Water Color by Vanderpoel, 1901.
Retrieved from Litchfield Historical Society

Vanderpoel's Portrait of Charlotte Siddall ca 1900. Retrieved from Litchfield Historical Society

SCHOOL OF ART.
DIRECTOR, MISS EMILY NOYES, New York City.
Miss E. Noyes, of New York, was Director of Art School at "Key-East Summer Institute" "'89," Key East, N. J., and is known as a successful teacher in Owego, N. Y., Princeton, N. J., and New York City. Instruction will be given in Charcoal Drawing and Sketching; Painting in Oils and Water Colors from Objects, Casts, and Nature; Still-Li'e and Life; China Painting; Tapestry Painting and Decorative Work on Textile Fabrics. The methods of teaching will be those in vogue in the Art Schools of New York and Paris.

Course Listing From 1891 Mt. Chautauqua

Signature Emily Vanderpoel, 1924

Charcoal or Crayon drawing on display at the Superintendent's house. ca. 1885
Courtesy Cumberland County Historical Museum

Professor W.M.R. French

Another "Tier 1" Art teacher in the Park in the summer of 1892 was Professor W.M.R. French, the first Director of the Art Institute of Chicago. The following summary appeared in the 1892 Mountain Chautauqua:

> Prof. W. M. R. French is the accomplished director of the celebrated Chicago Art School. He is, to begin with, a thorough artist, and seeks first of all to impart in his lectures information which will be helpful to those interested in art. He groups the great underlying principles and then illustrates them by rapidly drawn crayon sketches made in the presence of the audience. He talks all the time his fingers fly, and as if by magic beautiful landscapes, human figures, and many curious, grotesque, and funny things grow upon the paper. He has no superior in his line of work in the country. His entertainments will be a decided novelty to our patrons. He lectures twice, and the people will cry for more.

Prof. French from 1892 Mt. Chautauqua

Jennie White Kneass was a long-time summer art school teacher. From 1893 – 1910, she fired a kiln and had a studio in the Park. Jennie taught water color, oil, and porcelain painting. A course of 12 lessons cost $10. *"We had an old plate of our house, signed by Jennie White"*, recalled **Mrs. Meade Tibbins Foster**, former owner of the Clayton Cottage.

Painted Porcelain Plate of Clayton Cottage. Courtesy of Bob Boal.

Kindergarten

Mary Largent carries her book case along the Boardwalk to Kindergarten class, ca. 1903. Her Mother can be seen in the far right of the photo. Mary became a teacher; she taught English and Writing for more than 30 years.

The Mt. Lake Park Summer School of Kindergarten was conducted by **Miss Susan Plessner Pollock** and her assistant **Miss Minnie Daugherty**. It should be noted that the primary focus of this school was not to teach the children, although a small number of children were taught each year, but it was to train teachers how to teach Kindergarten. The "child students" were there so that the adult teachers in training could "practice" on them. From the West Va. Freeman newspaper, tuition (for the teachers) was $10.00, course materials, $1.00 and children were free.

Miss Minnie Daugherty and her kindergarten class, at the Hall of Philosophy around 1905.

"Miss Minnie always told us stories, and we'd just crowd around her, we just loved it," said Betty Randol. *"We had beads, colored paper, scissors, paste, everything they have in Kindergarten today."*

The classes were held in the Assembly Hall, and later, the Hall of Philosophy. Starting around 1906, Betty Randol attended the summer Kindergarten for four summers, she recalls *"(we had) so many teachers, you know, we all had a lot of attention, no wonder we loved it"*. With a student-teacher ratio around 1:1, or better, they would certainly get plenty of attention.

Elizabeth (Betty Leighton) Randol, from a 1951 yearbook photo. Betty would teach Home Economics in Garrett County for many years.

Nearly the entire **Pollock family** was involved in the introduction of Kindergarten in the United States. Susan Pollack's mother, Louise Plessner Pollock, was born in Germany in 1832 and she studied the Fröbel method of early education for children. Louise is cited as one of the first advocates for Kindergarten in the U.S.

Susan Pollock followed in her mother's footsteps and was the first U.S. citizen to graduate from the Fröbel institute in Berlin. She lectured on kindergarten training throughout the U.S. and, in 1874, founded the Kindergarten Normal Institute in Washington D.C. Susan Pollock operated the kindergarten summer school classes in Mt. Lake Park for more than 25 years. Susan wrote stories and articles for magazines such as Kindergarten-Primary magazine.

Susan Pollock

Louise Plessner Pollock

Born	29 October 1832 Erfurt
Died	24 July 1901 (aged 68) Skyland Resort

Retrieved from en.wikipedia.org/

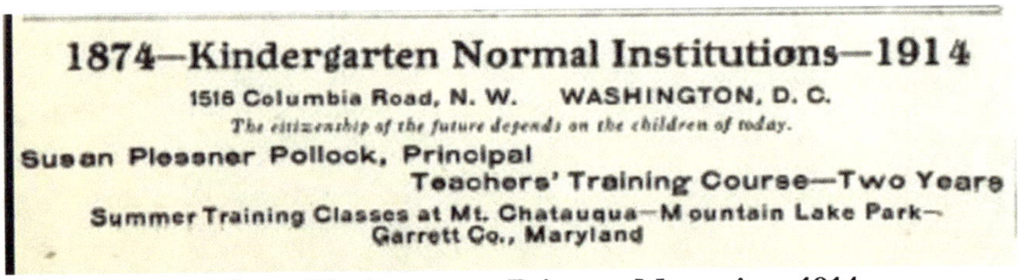

1874—Kindergarten Normal Institutions—1914
1516 Columbia Road, N. W.   WASHINGTON, D. C.
The citizenship of the future depends on the children of today.
Susan Plessner Pollock, Principal
Teachers' Training Course—Two Years
Summer Training Classes at Mt. Chatauqua—Mountain Lake Park—Garrett Co., Maryland

Advertisement from Kindergarten-Primary Magazine, 1914.

In 1892, Susan Pollock bought a lot and had a house built on what was "H" street (now Dave Turney Dr.) just below the Methodist Church.[9] It seems every few years she added a room or two to it. The house is still standing today, situated between the Chautauqua Cottage and the Methodist Church. At this location, it would be but a short walk each morning to the Hall of Philosophy to begin to teach the children and the teachers.

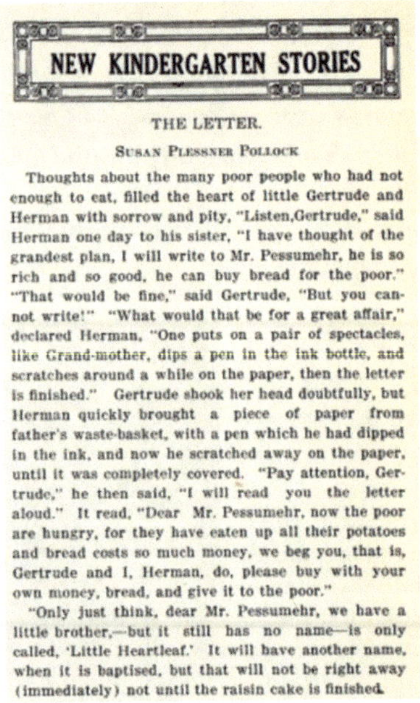

NEW KINDERGARTEN STORIES

THE LETTER.

SUSAN PLESSNER POLLOCK

Thoughts about the many poor people who had not enough to eat, filled the heart of little Gertrude and Herman with sorrow and pity. "Listen, Gertrude," said Herman one day to his sister, "I have thought of the grandest plan, I will write to Mr. Pessumehr, he is so rich and so good, he can buy bread for the poor." "That would be fine," said Gertrude, "But you cannot write!" "What would that be for a great affair," declared Herman, "One puts on a pair of spectacles, like Grand-mother, dips a pen in the ink bottle, and scratches around a while on the paper, then the letter is finished." Gertrude shook her head doubtfully, but Herman quickly brought a piece of paper from father's waste-basket, with a pen which he had dipped in the ink, and now he scratched away on the paper, until it was completely covered. "Pay attention, Gertrude," he then said, "I will read you the letter aloud." It read, "Dear Mr. Pessumehr, now the poor are hungry, for they have eaten up all their potatoes and bread costs so much money, we beg you, that is, Gertrude and I, Herman, do, please buy with your own money, bread, and give it to the poor."

"Only just think, dear Mr. Pessumehr, we have a little brother,—but it still has no name—is only called, 'Little Heartleaf.' It will have another name, when it is baptised, but that will not be right away (immediately) not until the raisin cake is finished."

Beginning of a story in Kindergarten-Primary Magazine, 1914.[10]

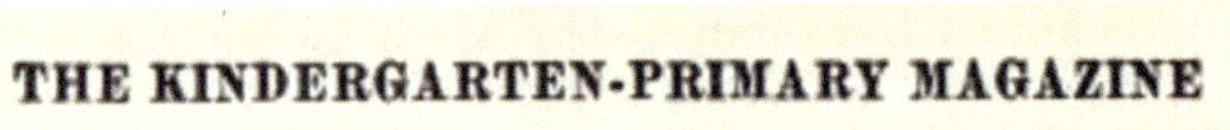

THE KINDERGARTEN-PRIMARY MAGAZINE

Susan wrote numerous children's stories, which were shared in magazines so that other Kindergarten teachers might use them in their classes.

Signature from Passport Application 1914

58

KINDERGARTEN, MOUNTAIN LAKE PARK CHAUTAUQUA.

The Chautauqua Magazine April-Sept 1902. Mary Largent front row, center (dark boots). Miss Minnie Daugherty thought to be in 3rd row, center.

Some other children that have been said to attend the kindergarten are Hugh Carr, Hallie and Harry Sanks, Gay Hayden, John Hayden, Ellen Hayden, Mrs. Mamie Carr Martin, the Miller sisters, Earl Enlow and his sisters, Miss Helen, Mrs. Gertrude Enlow Utterback; and Mrs. Lois Enlow Graeff.[11] Perhaps they are in the above picture?

After attending Kindergarten for four summers for four weeks each summer, Betty Randol was able to read and she was able to "skip" first grade. She reports that during her time, she was one of the few local residents that attend the school.[12]

School of Elocution
"…her method has saved many a public speaker from collapse." Prof. John B. Demotte, 1894

For more than two decades, **Miss Julia A. Orum** was the Principal of the Mt. Lake School of Elocution. It might be useful to review the definition of elocution: The Cambridge dictionary defines elocution as: *"the art of careful public speaking, using clear pronunciation and good breathing to control the voice"*. Prior to amplification, it was very important for a public speaker to learn how to project their voice in a dramatic manner, yet conserve their energy and protect their vocal chords. We can imagine the numerous preachers and lecturers that visited the Park were eager students of Miss Orum. She was also a renown public speaker in her own right.

Miss Julia Orum, from Werner's Magazine, 1894

Julia Orum came from a long line of true believers- the "Women of the Century" book states:[13] *"One of her maternal ancestors, Leonard Keyser, was burned at the stake for his faith, in 1527."* The same book further states that *"One of her paternal ancestors, Bartholomew Longstreth, of Yorkshire, Eng., was disinherited for becoming a Quaker and came to America in 1698."*

1. The natural form.
2. The fashion-plate form.

From Julia Orum's 1893 book <u>Voice Education</u>. In this book the author railed against the fashions of the day, pointing out the problems they caused with "Ladies" ability to speak in public.

The following recommendation of Julia Orum's book, "<u>Voice Education</u>", is from the Dec. 1894 issue of Werner's Magazine:

> Professor John B. De Motte expresses his appreciation in the following terms:
>
> "I feel that I am doing a public service in recommending Miss Julia A. Orum, her book, and her method of voice-development. She is inspiring. Her book contains the gist of all that is sensible in elocution, and <u>her method has saved many a public speaker from collapse</u>. Personally, she has taught me a number of things, any one of which would have been worth a journey round the world to get; and I know other persons who are equally indebted to her.
> John B. De Motte
> Cambridge Mass.

In the same article in Werner's Magazine, Julia's connection to the Woman's College of Baltimore is described, along with an endorsement from John F. Goucher:

> The Woman's College of Baltimore, one of the most progressive institutions of its kind in the world, after a careful survey of the whole field, selected Miss Orum as its teacher of elocution and vocal culture. In that institution last year she had over two hundred young ladies under her instruction, in addition to her classes in Philadelphia. At the close of her first year in that institution, Rev. Dr. Goucher gave her work the following hearty endorsement:
> Baltimore May 18, 1894

"Miss Julia A. Orum has been in charge of voice culture in the Woman's College of Baltimore during the present academic year. Her devotion to the work, her ability and skill in securing proper respiration, vocalization and expression have secured results which are entirely satisfactory. I heartily commend her to any who may desire the best development of their endowments in these directions

John F. Goucher
President of the Woman's College of Baltimore, 1894.

COTTAGE OF MISS JULIA ORUM, MOUNTAIN LAKE PARK.

Julia Orum and her cottage on "H" Street, now Dave Turney Drive. From Mountain Chautauqua, 1892.

Ultimately, Julia's health began to fail around 1900 and subsequently her property in the Park was sold off. The following Mortgagee's Sale notice, for the same property depicted here, appeared in the Republican paper on March 15, 1900. Miss Orum also had another substantial property built, the "Burlington," also known as the "Annex", next to the Deaconness Home on "H" Street. For more on that property, see the section on Boarding houses".

MORTGAGEE'S SALE
—OF VALUABLE—
REAL ESTATE.

Under and by virtue of a power of sale contained in a mortgage from Julia A. Orum to Julia W. Pearson bearing date the 9th day of September, 1893, and recorded in Liber E. Z. T. No. 25, folio 97, etc., one of the Mortgage Records of Garrett county, Maryland, and to me duly assigned as attorney for the purpose of foreclosure, default having been made therein, I will offer at public auction and sell to the highest bidder on

WEDNESDAY,

The 21st Day of March, 1900,

at the hour of 2 o'clock P. M., in front of the Court House in the town of Oakland, Maryland, all those two lots, pieces or parcels of land, situate at Mountain Lake Park, in said State, which on the plat of said Mountain Lake Park are known and described as

Lots Nos. 1020 and 1022

and being the same lots that were conveyed to the said Julia A. Orum by the Mountain Lake Park Association, the first by deed bearing date August 18th, 1890 recorded in Liber E. Z. T. No. 16, folio 188, and the second by deed bearing date September 30th, 1890, recorded in Liber E. Z. T. No. 16, folio 258, Land Records of Garrett county aforesaid.

Said lots are improved by a COMFORTABLE ONE-STORY DWELLING HOUSE AND NECESSARY OUTBUILDINGS AND CONVENIENCES and are very desirably located.

TERMS OF SALE—Cash on day of sale. Conveyancing at cost of purchaser.

FREDERICK A. THAYER,
Attorney and Assignee.

x

Chautauqua Performers

There can be a great deal of overlap between the Camp Meeting Evangelists, the Summer School Lecturers, and the "Performers". In this section we will highlight some of the showmen and troupes that traveled the Chautauqua circuit and visited the Park as performers. While many of these were high profile politicos and religious figures, just as often, they were musical groups and actors, and, in later years, the circuit took on more of a vaudeville feel. W.L. Davidson would book as many as 50 of these performers in a single 10 week season.

Captain Jack Crawford

Captain Jack, "The Poet Scout", was a popular speaker on the Chautauqua circuit in the 1890s and 1900s. Jack Crawford was a contemporary of Buffalo Bill Cody; he scouted with General Crook and he wrote several books with stories and poems about his western adventures. He was popular in the U.S. as well as his native Ireland.[1]

Captain Jack in the Park, 1904 by Amateur School of Photography. **A.A. Line Collection.**

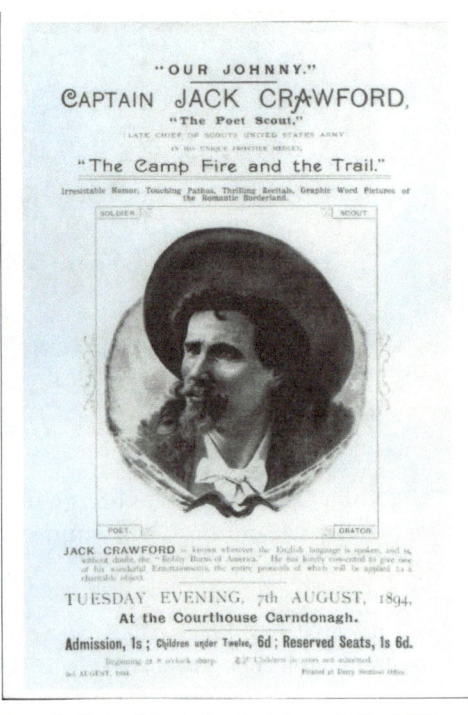

Capt. Jack, back in Ireland, giving a talk., 1894 Retrieved from Newstalk.com

Captain Jack was famous for his support of Temperance, which made him a good fit for Mt. Lake. Here he recounts a time when he carried a bottle of whiskey 400 miles to Buffalo Bill, as a favor:[2]

Captain Jack said:" What would you most like to have at this moment?" Bill replied: "A good big horn of old Bourbon." "Good enough ! You've struck it." said Jack. Buffalo Bill responded: " Git out — you can't fool me. What ! you carry a bottle of Bourbon four hundred miles?" Jack Responded: "Well, you know, Bill, I don't drink." "I know, and that's why I don't believe you would carry it so far." said Bill. Captain Jack said "And I wouldn't, but I promised a friend I would carry a parcel to you, and I've done it." Captain Jack pulled out the bottle in an instant. Bill snatched it while he was about to hold it up to show its color against the sky. "What the mischief are you doing ? " said Bill, concealing the bottle under his arm. " Do you want the whole command to pounce upon it like a pack of wolves?"

Captain Jack celebrating the end of the season. Advert from the Republican Newspaper, Aug., 1904.

Bean Soup at G.A.R. Day, Mt. Lake, ca. 1904 A.A. Line Collection, Cumberland County Historical Society.

The G.A.R. was a large veteran's organization similar to the American Legion of today.

President Taft at the Amphitheater

Certainly, one of the highlights of the all the Park's assemblies ever held was when President Taft traveled by train from Washington and spoke at the Mt. Lake Amphitheater on August 7, 1911. He had promised to speak during the 1911 season, initially in June, but Presidential events kept interfering and he finally found time on Monday, August 7th.

The excitement grew as reports of President Taft boarding his train came in from Washington. The Amphitheater, which seated up to 5000 people, would be filled to capacity, with 2000 more people waiting outside and hoping to catch a glimpse of the President.

President Taft arrived around 1:45pm and briefly toured Mt. Lake and Oakland before he was escorted to the Amphitheater, navigating the throngs of people. The subject of his speech was to be "International Peace".

The Republican, Front Page Aug. 3, 1911

Overflow Crowds

There is a story, often repeated, that, in order to accommodate Taft, the car the President was driven in needed to have a seat removed because of his ever-expanding girth. This story is validated in the Republican's Aug. 10, 1911 account of the President's visit:

Taft Day

To the very last there were reports abroad that the President was not coming. It is hard to tell whether this was because of the two former changes in program made by Mr. Taft, or whether it was attributable to our well known "gossipy spirit." Even Monday morning so late as 9 o'clock a report reached the office from one or two sources that the President had at the last minute decided not to come and the audiences would be disappointed.

A messenger was hurried off to the railway station and it was found that the President had been on the way for over an hour and was making great progress in our direction on his special train.

Two (excursion) trains from the West arrived, well filled and long before noon. People from Western Maryland, West Virginia and Pennsylvania also began to arrive by team and automobile.

The morning program, "The Melting Pot," by Miss Hobbs, was well attended. The President's train reached our station at exactly 1.45, and the local party consisting of the Board of Directors, the Annual Committee, and some fifteen or twenty of our citizens were taken to the train by about a dozen automobiles. Senator Harvey Sneicher had the honor of leading the procession on the President's brief tour around the Park and through Oakland. In the first car were the President, Major Butt, his military aide. Dr. Baldwin, President of the Association, and Senator Speicher, who drove his own car. The rest of the Presidential party was distributed throughout the local company and all enjoyed the visit and the drive very much. Lieut. E. S. West acted in an informal way as marshal. <u>An amusing incident of the drive suggestive of the physical proportions of our Chief was the necessity of stopping Senator Speicher's car and removing one of the seats in order that the President might have room.</u> The crowd assembled in the Amphitheatre was one of the largest it has ever known. The bands of Oakland and Keyser rendered a most delightful introductory concert listened to by perhaps a thousand or twelve hundred, and when the gates were thrown open to the public people poured in literally by the thousand. No estimate of the size of the crowd is under five thousand, and many have placed in as high as seven thousand.

When the President entered the vast throng arose at once and greeted him with tumultuous cheering. A patriotic quartette was sung by Mmes. Lumsden and Mardorf and Messrs. Clark and McCutchan. The service was opened by Dr. Charles W. Baldwin, of Baltimore, President of the Association, who in a few words introduced Senator Speicher who most tactfully refrained from making any speech but immediately presented and introduced Mr. Taft to the audience.

The President's speech was not what was expected by many of the audience, who looked for either the ordinary type of platform address or something that savored of political oratory, but it was a great speech in every sense of the term. The feeling was evident that the President was not talking to the people before him alone, but to the United States Senate, the whole people of the United States and in a very literal sense to the world at large. His appeal to the Methodist church to help in the forwarding of the cause of world peace was received with a storm of applause.

The address occupied hardly more than thirty minutes, and then young Mr. Ailer, because his car was somewhat more roomy, enjoyed the privilege of taking the President back to the train.

It was the plan that the special train should leave at once upon the return of the President, but strange as it may appear the newspaper men were delayed and their car had to exceed the speed limit in order to get them on the train at all.

TAFT'S PEACE PLEA

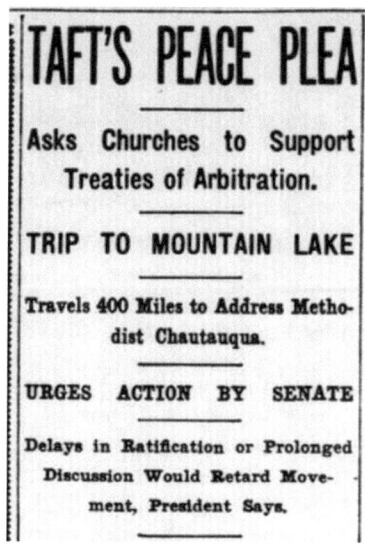

Asks Churches to Support Treaties of Arbitration.

TRIP TO MOUNTAIN LAKE

Travels 400 Miles to Address Methodist Chautauqua.

URGES ACTION BY SENATE

Delays in Ratification or Prolonged Discussion Would Retard Movement, President Says.

From The Evening Star
(Washington) Aug. 8 1911

President Taft stopping in Garrett County at a different time, on his way to Cincinnati, Ohio.

President Taft or Governor Fitzhugh Lee?

Every now and then, when one does research on a project such as this, unexpected things happen. Such was the case when the author was reviewing photographs in Carlisle Pa. The event concerns a photo that has been widely distributed, popularized in Mary Love's book, and is always cited as "President Taft at the Amphitheater".

In the Cumberland County Archives, I was requesting photos relating to Mt. Lake Park. The first picture the archivist brought out was the following picture. I said "Oh, that's President Taft at the Amphitheater". He said, "no, it says here it is Gov. Fitzhugh Lee". After much back and forth, he said he might need to update his records. When I went home, I searched out photos of Gov. Lee, and to my surprise, the "Taft" photo did appear to be Gov. Fitzhugh Lee. I called the archivist the next day and suggested he keep Gov. Lee in his records.

Both men definitely visited Mt. Lake and spoke at the Bashford Amphitheater; Gov. Lee on August 15, 1901, and President Taft on August 7, 1911.

Now, the reader is invited to review a following collection of pics, and try to determine the actual identity of the person in the photos at the Amphitheater. Besides the facial features matching, there are several other clues to examine: Gov. Lee was the nephew of Robert E. Lee and a renown Confederate General. That might explain the gentlemen in the confederate uniform on the righthand side of the picture. Clues to consider:

- Moustache turned down (Lee) vs Handlebar Moustache (Taft)
- Presence of Confederate Vet. (Lee was a former Confederate General)
- Tie clasp in Lee's formal 1895 portrait matches the tie clasp in the Amp Pictures
- The President's dark hair in a photo taken two months later.

The reader is invited to "stare and compare" and draw their own conclusion.

Photo included in the book, <u>Once Upon a Moutaintop</u> by Mary I. Love, this copy from the Cumberland County Museum, Carlisle, Pa. A.A. Line on far left.

From en.wikipedia.org/wiki/Fitzhugh_Lee

The photo was taken at the exit of the Amphitheater and was taken just prior to, or just after, the photo on the following page. This photo was found in the Cumberland County Museum in Carlisle, Pa. and is labeled "Gov. Fitzhugh Lee at Mt. Lake Park". A.A. Line from the Amateur school of Photography is in the left of the picture.

A Great Day at Mountain Lake Park.

In the nineteen years of its history the Mountain Chautauqua has never presented a stronger program than will be given on August 15th. Gen. Fitzhugh Lee, the idol of the South, will lecture in the afternoon. Capt. Richmond Pearson Hobson, whose heroic act in the sinking of the Merrimac at the mouth of Santiago harbor is one of the immortal acts of the Spanish-American war, will lecture in the morning. The desire to see

The Republican Aug. 8, 1901

Governor Lee was a familiar figure in Mt. Lake Park. In 1900 and 1901, he rented "Altamont", a summer cottage owned by Mrs. Hardy on "M" street. Photos of Mrs. Hardy's cottage appear in the chapter on Cottages.

Another Photo found in the Cumberland County Museum, Carlisle, Pa. A.A. Line Collection This photo is titled, "Gov. Fitzhugh Lee in Mt. Lake Park." This photo was taken within seconds of the previous photo. A.D. Naylor is thought to be next to the children on the right.

President Taft on Nov. 1 1911, in Morgantown, just 2 months after his visit to Mt. Lake. Note Taft's dark hair.

From Lee 1895 Photo, previous page.

From Photo, above

Regardless of the readers conclusion concerning the identity of the person in the picture, both Lee and Taft spoke at the amphitheater. Mt. Lake Park did not lose a President so much as gain a Governor!

Rev. Anna H. Shaw

Another popular lecturer on the Chatauqua circuit was Rev. Anna H. Shaw, a medical doctor and a leader in the women's suffrage movement. As shown in the illustration, she spoke on a variety of subjects, including women's suffage. Rev. Shaw visited Mt. Lake many times over the years.

Retrieved from the University of Iowa Libraries/ digital.lib.uiowa.edu

SUBJECTS

"The New Man"
"The Fate of Republics"
"The Power of the Incentive"
"The New Democratic Ideal"
"The American Home"
"Colonization and Civilization"
"The Relation of Woman's Ballot to the Home"
"Woman Suffrage Essential to a True Republic"
"The Temperance Problem"
(Sunday) "The Heavenly Vision"
(Sunday) "Strength of Character"

MARY CARNELL, Photographer.

REV. ANNA H. SHAW

> The concluding address in the Brooklyn Institute series on "The Position of Women" was delivered at the Art Gallery by the Rev. Anna Howard Shaw of Philadelphia. She interested an audience by speaking on "The Political Status of Women." — *The Brooklyn Eagle, N. Y.*

Governor. Lloyd Lowndes, Jr.

Maryland Gov. Lowndes was a featured speaker in 1896. The Governor hailed from Alleghany County and was influential in Garrett and Allegheny politics. He spoke on G.A.R. day; a crowd of nearly 4000 had gathered, and this was before the Amphitheater was built. These G.A.R. days were times of reconciliation for a nation still attempting to recover from the devastation of the Civil War. The Aug. 27, 1896 Republican newspaper captures the scene as the crowd gathered:

Gov. Lowndes Courtesy of Md. State Archives

> *Three front rows of seats and a portion of the platform were reserved for the veterans of the two armies, designated respectively for those who wore the blue, and those who wore the gray. There may have been two hundred of these "survivors" of the great war in the hall. They were a most interesting group, gray-headed, gray-bearded men, who seemed to be conscious of something that distinguished them from the crowd around them; but all so much alike in form and feature, and cult, that had it not been for an occasional grey coat, or Grand Army badge, no one would have known whether they had fought under the stars and stripes, or under the stars and bars, while they were in repose.*

Civil War Vets at Mt. Lake Park

Professor Thomas Dinsmore was a well-reviewed showman, providing "Lectures with Experiments'. It appears Dr. Dinsmore attempted to use experiments to prove that life could not be created by science. This subject was likely a comfort to the Mt. Lake Park crowds.

DR. THOS. DINSMORE,
Lectures with Experiments.

From a 1900 Mountain Chautauqua Poster

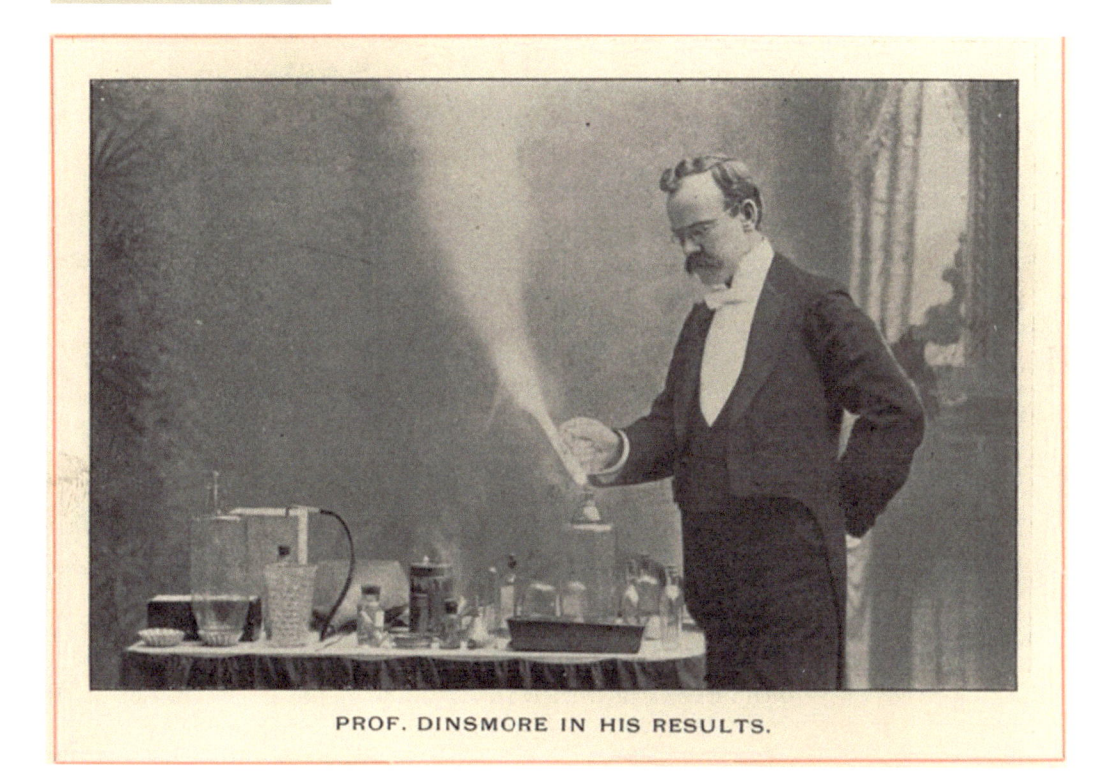

PROF. DINSMORE IN HIS RESULTS.

The lecture by Prof. Dinsmore was well attended and proved to be both interesting and instructive. When it came to the Professor's demonstration that it would be impossible to create life by any combination of chemicals and electricity, the audience was fully satisfied.—*Republican, Tipton, Ia.*

University of Iowa Libraries | digital.lib.uiowa.edu/tc

The performers in the next photo below are a bit of a mystery. The photo, recovered from the A.A. Line collection in Carlisle, Pa. is captioned: "Dr. J. H. Morgan with a group of people dressed in Arab costumes, Mt. Lake Park, Maryland." Dr. Morgan was Dean of the Summer Schools and he is in the center of the back row, with a white beard and cap. Another aspect of this photo that raises unanswered questions is: why are the people on the left of the photo covered in white, and the ones on the right covered in a darker color?

Dr. J.H Morgan outside the Amphitheater, ca. 1901. From the A.A. Line Collection.[3]

P. VON FINKLESTEIN MAMREOV,
A Native of Jerusalem.

LECTURE TOPICS.
1. Fallaheen, or Farmers of Palestine.
2. City and Domestic Life in Jerusalem.
3. Bedouins of Arabia and Palestine.
4. Jews of Jerusalem.
5. Ana Hoo Yasuh I'Naasree; or, I am He, Jesus of Nazareth.
6. New Light on Lives of Patriarchs.
All given in beautiful and native costumes. One of the most unique, attractive and helpful entertainments now on the lecture platform. Engagements can be made for lectures by applying to Slayton Lyceum Bureau, Central Music Hall, Chicago, Ill.; or Lincoln Building, New York, N. Y.

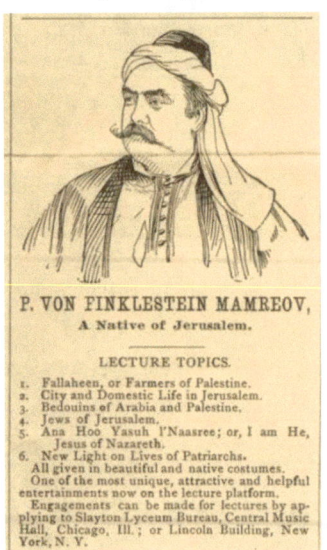

In reviewing acts on the Chautauqua circuit, we find an advertisement in the Park's 1892 Mountain Chautauqua (left) that may be describing this troupe and their performances.

The Mamreov Troupe performed in 1891 in Mt. Lake Park.[4] and again in 1909. This photo likely dates somewhere in between and Dr. Morgan looks like he did around 1901.

The man standing in the right-center of the photo is likely Mr. P. Von Finklestein Mamreov, a "native of Jerusalem", as seen in the illustration. The "Lecture Topics" in this advert appear to align with the composition of the troupe. Mr. Peter Von Finklestein Mamreov and his relatives published a book, "Jesus of Nazareth" in 1894. We can imagine what a sensation these performers would cause for the local folks, many of whom had not traveled beyond the surrounding counties. The other thing we can speculate on is, Dr. J.H. Morgan must have been an easygoing supporter, to participate in the performance himself.

There were many popular music acts over the years, such as the Royal Hungarian Gypsy Orchestra, the Lyric Concert Company, and the Philharmonic Quartette; they would often play daily; there were also acts that that had a measure of novelty. Two such acts were the famous whistler, Miss Laura Mcmanis, and the English Bell Ringers.

Miss Laura McManis—Truly called the "Nightingale" among whistlers; a thorough artist whose birdlike melodies greatly charm and please. Miss McManis is the young lady who created such a sensation at the National Encampment of the G. A. R., with her sweet and unique music. Her sister, Miss Alice, an accomplished musician, accompanies her on the piano.

MISS LAURA MCMANIS.

From the 1896 Mt. Chautauqua

English Hand-Bell Ringers—The reigning novelty of the year. Something entirely new to our patrons. Four young men, trained musicians, making delightful music on 134 hand-bells. They play many popular airs in a charming manner. Their imitation of English Cathedral bells is remarkably realistic. The sweet chiming of the bells, the tender notes of the zither, the merry twanging of the banjo make up an entertainment well calculated to drive dull care away.

ENGLISH HAND BELL RINGERS.

Many hundreds of other lecturers, readers, showman (and women), and musicians made appearances over the years. Two more of these were William Jennings Bryan and Sam Jones.

Ed Lewis recalled, *"I remember my father taking me up to shake hands with Mr. Bryan. I changed my opinion of him later."* Presumably Mr. Lewis is referring to Mr. Bryan's promotion of the literal interpretation of the Bible and his subsequent role as the prosecutor in the Scopes anti-evolution trial.

Sam Jones drew crowds in excess of 4000 people and commanded up to $300.00 per performance.[5] After around 1912, as America's tastes in travel, education, and entertainment began to change, the crowds started to dwindle and it later became more and more difficult to finance the operation.

Photos on next two pages, Kindergartner, Capt. Jack Crawford, Martha Friend Weimer, Martin's store.

8 - TIME LINE OF EVENTS 1881 - 1921

1881	Founders Make Their Move	Form Association, Buy Land, B & O Agreements
1882	Initial Building	1st Buildings, Camp Meetings, Mt. Lake Hotel
1882	Mt. Lake	Mr. Burley builds the Lake (approx. 20 acres)
1882	1st Post Office, Depot	A.R. Sperry builds combined P.O., depot
1883	Jennie Smith & Family	Extended Family Arrives, Grace Cottage, Dining,
1883	Ice Harvest	Mr. Burley builds a small Ice house, west of Lake
1884	Crystal Spring	Drive to Crystal Spring completed
1884	Chautauqua Emerges	C.L.S.C. Relocates from Pa., 1st Summer Schools
1888	Community Chartered	Assoc. transfers road maintenance to Community.
1888	Faith Home	Faith Home / Hamilton Hall built
1890	Davidson & Rudisill	Take the Mountain Chautauqua to a new level
1890	Hotel Dennett	Mr. A.W. Dennett builds his hotel
1890	Telegraph	Extended from Depot to Superintendent's office
1893	Columbian	Columbian Hotel built by Adam Howell (Smith)
1894	Association expands	Buildout of Lake, plans for Hall of Philosophy
1894	Ice House & side track	Big Ice House built & side track, west side of lake
1894	1st Electric Lights	Electric strung from Oakland, grove lighted
1896	Hall of Philosophy	C.L.S.C., Kindergarten, Lectures, Vesper Services
1898	Water, Sewer	Initial attempts at sewer, water distribution
1898	Ice Plows for Horses	Mr. Rudisill buys Ice Plows for Ice Harvesting
1899	Amphitheater Plans	$6000 approved for Amphitheater
1899	Rev. Thompson	Death of Rev. John Thompson
1900	Ticket Office & Amp.	Amphitheater & Ticket Office built

Time Line of Events 1881 - 1921

1900	Electric Lighting	Initial Electric Plant in Mt. Lake
1900	Baseball fields	Moved to just below the dam
1900	Bethel Church	Built, along with Parsonage
1901	Gov. Fitzhugh Lee	Gov. Lee speaks at Amp; rents Altamont Cottage
1903	Chautauqua Grows	Up to 25 "Departments" (areas of study)
1903	The Colonial	Weimer Brothers build the Colonial
1904	Winter	50 Families wintering over in Mt. Lake (Republican 10-6-04)
1905	Goucher	Proposes to sell his stock for $10,000 – No Sale
1905	Goucher	Declines Position of President of Association
1906	Railroad	~1906, Free passes and R.R. Rebates eliminated
1906	Civic Club	Civic Club builds the tennis court /bowling alley
1907	Automobiles	Assoc. passes regulation limiting speed of cars through Park
1907	Post office burns	Store burned out as well, fire of suspicious origin
1908	Big Ice House burns	Fire of suspicious origins; new Ice House built
1909	Dennett Hotel	In ruins, after a few years of neglect (a.k.a. Overlook)
1911	President Taft	Speaks at the Amphitheater, nearly 7000 on hand
1911	Amphitheater fire	Electrical fire in Amp., building saved.
1911	New Post office	New P.O. built, set back from the R.R. tracks.
1912	W.L. Davidson	Chautauqua Superintendent resigns after 22 years.
1912	Attempted Sale	Association wants to Sell Park for $137,000 – No Sale
1920	Big Fire	Fire destroys Assembly house, 4 other Cottages
1921	Association assets sold	Sold to Board of Foreign Missions; end of era
1931	*Town Established*	*Mt. Lake Park incorporated, Mayor & Town Council*

9 - BLACK PEOPLE OF MT. LAKE PARK

Any attempt to describe Black people's experience in Mt. Lake in a book such as this is bound to fall short. The information and pictures uncovered are limited and incomplete. And, although the best historic sources are nearly always primary, first-person accounts, most everything found thus far is provided by White individuals.

As described throughout this book, the Park was founded by M.E. Ministers. Historically, the split of the M.E. Church and the origins of African Methodist Episcopal Church (A.M.E.) can be traced to the discrimination that black parishioners experienced, such as a requirement for separate seating, in the early 1800s.[1] Leading up to the Civil War, the M.E. church and it's Ministers, particularly in the North, were strongly opposed to slavery.[2] This apparently did not extend so far as to encourage the complete integration of worshiping and other religious-based activities. This was not uncommon during this era. This information is provided as a context when reviewing the history of Black people in Mt. Lake.

There were numerous Black people living and working in Garrett County in the late 1800s.

In 1966, E.R. O'Donnell said,[3] *"Around the turn of the century, and before that time, there were quite a few black people in and around Mt. Lake and Loch Lynn Heights, both permanent residents and the summer help."*

A quick review of the 1900 census data shows that 128 people of color (119 Black, 9 Mixed Race) lived in Garrett County.

This number does not capture the full picture as there were many black people that came to the area for summer work in the hotels, on farms, on the railroad and the like. For example, in August of 1903, nearly 40 black workers from Mt. Lake held a "society dance" in a hall in Deer Park.[4]

The year-round Black residents stayed put but the summer workers moved on, likely finding winter-time work off the mountain. It is also known that many of the Park's wealthier cottage owners employed blacks as domestic servants, drivers, and gardeners; some of the home owners brought these workers with them during their summer residencies. The local Black citizens in Oakland, Loch Lynn and beyond also visited the Park during the summer. (see below)

Colored Society Notes.
Mr. John Danridge, of Wheeling, is here on a visit to his father and sisters.
Mrs. Baker Banks, Mrs. James Truly and Aunt Harriett Dunmark, were at the Park Sunday afternoon.
Miss Ida Dunmark is still very sick.
Mr. W. G. Glover has opened a barber shop on Main street. Work will be attended to promptly. Stop in boys and have a shave.

From the Republican July, 9, 1894.

Aunt Harriet Dunmark has gone to Mountain Lake Park to spend a few weeks.

From the Republican Aug. 9, 1894 Sometimes the Dunmark name was spelled "Denmark".

For several months in 1894, the Republican newspaper had a column titled "Colored Society Notes." Here the Black population's comings and goings, events, illnesses, visits, etc., are described in much the same way as any other community, such as Deer Park or Grantsville. These columns offer some insight into Black society in Garrett County around the turn of the century. At the same time, numerous articles are found with derogatory slights and negative stereotypes regarding Black people.

Morgantown Band at Mt. Lake Park ca 1890. Note the 3 unidentified Black men in this photo. From their attire, they appear to be food workers. Courtesy West Virginia and Regional History Center, West Virginia University Libraries.

A visiting preacher of color described in the "Camp Meeting" Chapter was Amanda Berry Smith. This is the only active Black preacher identified thus far in Mt. Lake during this era. (Although Rev. William H. Walker, likely of the soon-to-be A.M.E. church in Oakland is listed as living in Mt. Lake in the 1900 census.). Mrs. Smith was a well-known evangelist, she aligned with the holiness movement, which espoused the doctrine of sanctification or "second blessing". This movement attracted portions of the Methodist and Quaker denominations, among others, and was a central component to the Mt. Lake Camp Meeting experiences. In her autobiography, Amanda Smith described traveling the country and often seemed to be the only Black person at some of the Camp Meetings. She was able to navigate between the M.E. and the A.M.E. churches, and was well respected by both.

Born into slavery, Amanda Berry had very little education, but she rose above it and traveled the world, doing all she could to spread the Christian faith. She writes of her limited schooling, in Long Green, Maryland, in her 1893 autobiography:

> *Three months of schooling was all I ever had. That was at a school for whites; though a few colored children were permitted to attend. To this school my brother and I walked five and a half miles each day, in going and returning, and the attention we received while there was only such as the teacher could give after the requirements of the more favored pupils had been met.*

Amanda Smith at a Camp Meeting in Washington State, ca. 1897.[5] She often found herself the only person of color at these Camp Meetings.

This excerpt from the "Birds-eye view of Mt. Lake" map depicts the Washington Inn, at the Northeast corner of Philadelphia and K street.[6] According to the oral histories collected by Mary Love, in the smaller house just next to the hotel, lived a large extended family of Black people. The people in this family are said to have worked at the different hotels and businesses in the Park. These buildings were torn down in the 1960s; this is the area known as Veterans Park today.

From various sources identified in this chapter and this book, we can begin to identify the types of work Black people did around Mt. Lake. There are references of specific people identified in the following occupations:

- Barbers — Richard Moore
- Laundress — Martha McGuffin
- Livery/Wagon drivers — Jack McGuffin
- A Preacher — Amanda Smith (Also Rev. W.H. Walker)
- Farm Workers — Charles Washington
- Waiters — Unknown, picnic photo subsequent page
- Kitchen workers — Assembly House, photo previous page

- Nannies/ "Nurses"   Cottage-based, such as Ella Jackson
- Road Graders   Jack McGuffin
- Workers at a Store   John Cole (Richardson's store)[7]
- Ice Harvesters   From oral accounts
- Lumber Yard   Workers

While there is some variety above, there was some work from which Black people appear to be explicitly excluded. The following "help wanted" advertisement of the Chautauqua Hotel ran in the Republican newspaper for several weeks in 1899:

> **Wanted for Hotel Chautauqua, Mountain Lake Park.**
>
> 4th, Ten good white waiter girls and chamber maids, and two white or colored laundry women for hotel linen.   Address,
>   T. D. RICHARDS,
> 2-4   Germantown, Md.

A couple of year-round Black families are highlighted, below.

One Black family that lived and worked in the Park, from the 1890s until at least 1920 was the **Moore family**.[8] Richard Moore, Sr. was a barber at the hotels in Mt. Lake and Loch Lynn for many years. The hotels where Mr. Moore was specifically known to have his business were the Mt. Lake Hotel, the Chautauqua Hotel, and Hicks House in Loch Lynn. Mr. Moore's wife was Maggie M. (Jones) from Fairmont, and his daughter was Annabelle Moore. His son, Richard Moore, Jr. attended Mt. Lake Park's public school. Richard, Jr. ultimately attended Fairmont State College in Fairmont, W.Va.

> PATRONIZE
> RICHARD W. MOORE'S
> **BARBER SHOP.**
> Mountain Lake Park Hotel.
> First-Class Work for First-Class People by a First-Class Barber.

From 1911 Mt. Lake Chautauqua Brochure.

Maggie M (Jones) was a cousin of Mrs. Hattie Harper, of Frostburg, Maryland. At times, Maggie's mother, Mariah Jones, lived in Loch Lynn. She died there and is buried in Oakland Cemetery.[9]

Jack and Martha McGuffin were longtime residents of Mt. Lake and Loch Lynn. Jack was born in 1867 in Augusta County, Virginia and Martha was born in Maryland in 1864. Jack was one of the wagon drivers during Jack Echard's excursions. He drove an eight-seated spring wagon with four horses.[10] He drove visitors to Swallow Falls, Conneway Tower (backbone mtn), and the Boiling Spring near Deer Park.

In 1914, it is reported that Jack McGuffin had purchased four additional lots, two on each side of his home premises. Because this was reported in the Mt. Lake column of the Republican, it is assumed this house and lots were in Mt. Lake, but the specific location is not known. In later years, they are identified as living in Loch Lynn.[11] In 1915, the McGuffin's are listed as annual subscribers to the Republican newspaper.[12] In census records, both are listed as capable of reading and writing. In the 1910 census, Martha McGuffin's occupation is listed as a laundress.

In 1916, again in the Mt. Lake column, Jack was reported as "doing good work with the road machine."[13] This would imply that he was employed by the Mt. Lake Community Association because they were responsible for the roads at that time. By 1930, Jack and Martha were living in Loch Lynn, in a house they owned on Seneca Ave. and Jack was working at the Pea Cannery located in Loch Lynn.[14] Jack and Martha both died in the early 1930s, Jack on Dec. 31, 1931. The exact date of Martha's death is not known but believed to be before 1935. Jack is buried in a cemetery in Pleasant Valley.

A picnic near Allegheny Drive, ca. 1920. Courtesy of Sarah Haynes

As the Park activities and the other large hotels began to wind down in the 1920s, there was also a decline in the number of Black people living and working in the area. In 1930, the census records indicate just two Black people living in district seven, which makes up Mt. Lake and Loch Lynn. Jack and Martha McGuffie were described by E.O. O'Donnell as the last Black people living in Mt. Lake or Loch Lynn in the 1930s. Today, there are once again numerous people of color living in the area.

10 - THE ASSOCATION BUILDINGS

The founders knew that building public spaces would be a key ingredient for the success of the summer resort. Immediately after signing the papers to purchase "Hoyes pasture", they set about making the accommodations for the 1882 season.[1] The first association-owned buildings to be built included the Tabernacle, and the Mt. Lake Hotel, the Hotel being sold to Mr. H.H. Van Meter at the end of the 1882 season. Subsequent association buildings included the Assembly Hall, just in front of the Tabernacle, the Superintendent's Office and house (two different buildings), Assembly House (a boarding house) and cottage rentals, the Hall of Philosophy, the Bowling Alley and Tennis Courts, (built by the women's civic club, the "Crystal Spring Natatorium and Amusement Corp.") and then, ultimately the Bashford Amphitheater, Book Store, and Ticket office.

Several of these buildings align with the names of the buildings in the "Mother Chautauqua" in Lake Chautauqua, New York. In New York, as in the Park, there was a Tabernacle, Auditorium, Hall of Philosophy, Book Store, and a Deaconess home. (The Mt. Lake Deaconess home is covered in another chapter.)

We will review these places in a semi-chronological order, so we start with the Tabernacle.

Tabernacle (1 on map)

The tabernacle was also known as the Auditorium, and later, after the Amphitheater was built, as the "old Auditorium", this to distinguish it from the "new Auditorium" which was the Amphitheater. It was one of the first structures completed in 1882 and was "ground zero" for the camp meetings, schools, and performances until the late 1890s.

The structure was "open air" on the sides, with the side walls covered by heavy canvas for shelter, when the summer rainstorms hit. The tabernacle is surrounded by the "grove", a wide expanse of large oaks, with benches and chairs scattered among the trees.

The Auditorium, Mtn Lake Park, Md.

Assembly Hall (Left) and the Tabernacle (Right). Assembly Hall was built in 1883 by Mr. J.M. Jarboe. The Hall hosted classes, art studios, lectures, and later, a gym on the 2nd floor.

The three signs in the Tabernacle are the "three mottos" of the Chautauqua Literary Scientific Circle (C.L.S.C) The motto on the left is: ***"We study the Word & Works of God".*** The sign on the right, ***"Never be Discouraged"***. The sign in the center of the stage reads "***Let us keep the Heavenly Father in the Midst***". This phrase can be traced to the very origins of the Chautauqua study movement, when, in 1879, at Lake Chautauqua, the Chautauqua Literary Scientific Circle (C.L.S.C.)

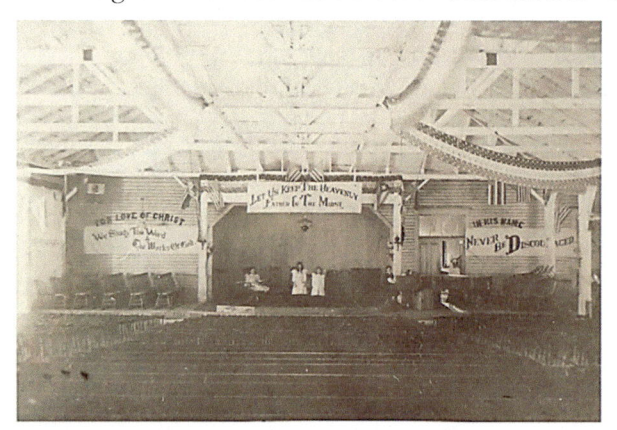

Interior View of the Tabernacle, ca. 1890

was organized.[2] The second member to sign up for that initial study circle was Dr. Vail. Dr. Vail signed his name to the roll and said "Let us keep our heavenly father in the Midst". Dr. Vail was answered, "That shall be our motto". From that first study circle grew hundreds of groups and thousands of students, all over the world, including a C.L.S.C in Mt. Lake Park. The C.L.S.C held formal graduation exercises on "Recognition Day", in the Tabernacle; when a group of students completed their (up to) four year course of studies. The graduates would form up at the Hall of Philosophy, then March through the arches that led to the tabernacle and receive their "seals."[3]

Over the decades, the Tabernacle went through a few incarnations; it was expanded in the 1890s, to accommodate up to 1500 people. It saw a little less use when the Bashford Amphitheatre was built in 1900. In 1941, it was destroyed by fire; it was rebuilt and then the roof collapsed from the weight of snow in the 1960s. It was rebuilt yet again and still stands today.

Mt. Lake Hotel (2 on map)

The Mt. Lake Hotel was the first Hotel built in the Park, it was commissioned by the Association, with the initial structure completed by July, 1882. The Association contracted with a local builder, Mr. James M. Jarboe, to build the hotel and, later that summer, leased the Hotel to Mr. Harry Van Meter of Philadelphia. Mr. Jarboe would go on to build many of the Park's Cottages and Boarding houses, several of which still remain today.

Some of the owner/operators over the years, included Mr. Van Meter, Mrs. Virginia Stine, Mr. L.T. Yoder (founding association shareholder and waterworks operator), W.Creed Dunnington and Miss June Dunnington (Grimes).

The Hotel was the first to be built and the last to go; it was in continuous (summer) operation until the mid-1960s. At that time, all the furniture and removable building materials were auctioned off. Many people that lived in Mt. Lake bought something. As we visit the various cottages today, remnants of the Hotel are found all over town; we can find beds, the front desk (seen in the postcard below), rocking chairs, plates and china, washstands, and porch railings.

In 1895, a secondary two-story building was erected behind the hotel; the second floor had 8 bedrooms, used for "servants" quarters. On the first floor was a bakery, storeroom and laundry. In the basement a large boiler was installed for heating the complex. The estimated cost for this addition was $2500.[4]

Builder James M. Jarboe

Mt. Lake Hotel, ca. 1900.

Hotel Lobby

Association Buildings

Marketing Flyer, 1897

Rare Interior View, Parlor

Closer View of the entrance, Mt. Lake Hotel, ca. 1895. We have no idea what the people are looking at. Photo from A.A. Line Collection, Cumberland County Historical Society. Note the fire escape ladders.

Association Buildings

Original Porch Railing at Mt. Lake Hotel

Same Porch Railing now re-used at a Cottage on E street. Courtesy of Mimi and Dave Degrafft

Plate and Sugar Bowl, Courtesy of Mimi and Dave Degrafft.

Dear Miss Roderick! -Am very sorry but I am all vacancies filled. If any of my girls disappoint, I shall be glad to take you. Very Truly Yours, Miss June Dunnington. 1917. Miss Dunnington is telling Miss Roderick that all her job openings are filled.

1917 Post Card from June Dunnington

Miss Dunnington's father, W. Creed Dunnington operated the hotel at that time. June A. Dunnington would go on to operate the Mt. Lake Hotel for many years, with her partner, Mrs. Lillian Davis. June Dunnington married William D. Grimes of Pittsburgh;[5] her daughter, Martha Grimes, wrote several novels set in Mt. Lake and in the Mt. Lake Hotel. The Dunnington's hosted elaborate parties at the Mt. Lake Hotel, with one 1920 New Year's Eve party including up to 500 guests.[6]

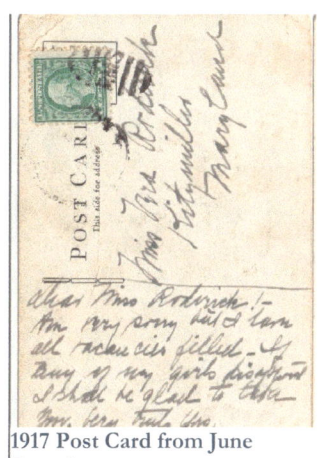

Association Buildings

Bed from the Mt. Lake Hotel Courtesy of Sarah Haynes

Waitresses Mt. Lake Hotel

Rocker from Mt. Lake Hotel, Courtesy of Sarah Haynes.

The hotel initially had approximately 25 rooms, and was expanded to around 47 rooms before 1891. In 1892, the Hotel size was again doubled, bringing the total number of rooms to nearly 100. The hotel business carried on, through the changes (including dancing) and decline of the 40s, 50s, and 1960s. Mt. Lake resident Dave Degrafft and his wife, Mimi, were some of the last guests in the mid-sixties. *"It was just worn out by then, everything worn out"*, he said.

It was finally closed in the mid-60s and torn down in 1968.

1934 Advert. As the Association lost its grip and the Park became a Town, things like dancing and drinking became tolerated. Too late for most of the hotels, but Mt. Lake Hotel carried on.

The music is silent. The warm lights are gone. The empty shell of the Mt. Lake hotel is razed in 1968.

The Superintendent's Office (3 on Map)

This, perhaps the most ornate of all the Park buildings, the "Super's office", also known as the Association Office, was completed in the Spring of 1884, and served as an office for the Association. This building was located directly in front of the Assembly Hall and Tabernacle. The superintendent had responsibility for the day-to-day operations and construction of the Park and was also immersed in the marketing and printing of newsletters and flyers as well as groundskeeping and rentals. In 1890, the B & O ran a telegraph line from the office to the Train Depot. This enabled near constant communication.[7]

The office building also provided a location for summer school classes, we can see several of the students and faculty of the Art, Photography and other classes in the picture below.

Superintendent's Office, ca. 1885. Note the children playing in the right-hand corner. Many of the people in this picture are students and teachers of the School of Photography. Dr. Himes, center-right, standing. Albert Line, left in front of stairs. School Dean Dr. J.H. Morgan sitting on stairs. Art teachers or students on left porch near easel. Jared Young stated that his father, Rev. J.B. Young, took this picture as he was attending this photography school. **This copy was collected from the Cumberland County Historical Society. It is part of the A.A. Line collection.**

Side view of "Super's" office

View down F street prior to 1910. Superintendent's Office in the distance.

The building no longer stands. It is not known when the Office was torn down.

The Assembly House (4 on Map)

ASSEMBLY HOUSE,
Mountain Lake Park, Md.
TERMS REASONABLE.
Pleasantly located, near Auditorium, good shade, large verandas. Good table and service.
MRS. S. O. SAWYER, Manager.

The Assembly house was built in 1885 and first served as a dining hall and later a boarding house, owned by the Association. In 1889, the Association changed its name from the "Park Dining Hall" to "Assembly House". It was located on E Street and for some number of years it was operated by Mrs. S.O. Sawyer. Often, groups performing at the Chautauqua would stay there. There were also four small cottages operated in conjunction with this house. The Assembly house and the cottages were destroyed by fire on March 31, 1920.[8] The fire was started after some workers were burning leaves; this was the biggest fire experienced in the Park. Five buildings were completely destroyed, and several more were damaged.

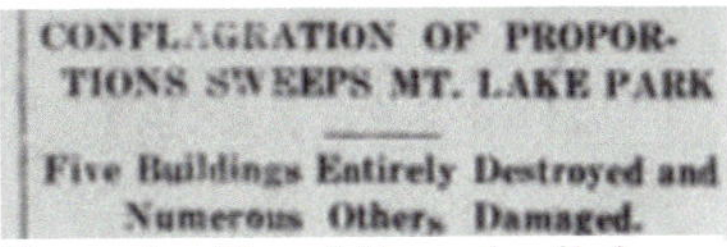

CONFLAGRATION OF PROPORTIONS SWEEPS MT. LAKE PARK

Five Buildings Entirely Destroyed and Numerous Others Damaged.

From the Republican April, 1, 1920.

Morgantown Band at Assembly House ca. 1890 Courtesy West Virginia and Regional History Center, West Virginia University Libraries

Hall of Philosophy (5 on Map)

The following notice was found in the 1884 Mt. Lake Messenger:

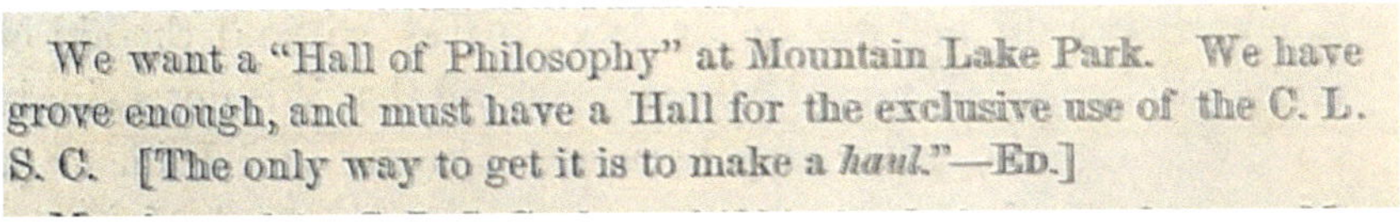

We want a "Hall of Philosophy" at Mountain Lake Park. We have grove enough, and must have a Hall for the exclusive use of the C. L. S. C. [The only way to get it is to make a *haul*."—ED.]

From the 1884 Mt. Lake Messenger

Hall of Philosophy
Chautauqua, N.Y.

As early as 1884, the members of the Park C.L.S.C. were requesting their own "Hall of Philosophy" to emulate the building at "Mother Chautauqua" in New York. Their request would come to fruition 12 years later, but it was not exclusively used by the C.L.S.C.

Illustration from the 1906 MLP Birds-eye View Map, shows the front entrance of the Hall of Philosophy.

Plans for the Hall of Philosophy were drawn up in 1895 and construction completed in 1896. The building was constructed with sloping floors and seating to provide everyone a line-of-sight view. The building housed lectures, readings, summer school courses, kindergarten, Vesper Services, and musical performances of all varieties.

Hall of Philosophy Hour.

The 4 o'clock hour in the Hall of Philosophy, has for several seasons, been given to lectures of high literary value. The experiment has more than justified the faith of the Superintendent of Instruction in the need and acceptability of such work. Last year the Hall was crowded daily with thoughtful people who gave unstinted approval to the work. This year the service has been arranged to take the place of the afternoon lecture which was formerly a part of the regular Chautauqua program, but for the sake of giving a little time for rest and recreation, the transfer was made to the Hall of Philosophy and the hour placed a little later in the cool of the day.

This year at the Hall of Philosophy, special courses covering a week each, will be given by prominent and successful lecturers and entertainers.

Reading Hours by Miss Cora Mel Patten and Mrs. W. E. Lewis, and lectures on economic questions by Prof. J. W. Crook.

Story Telling Hour.

In charge of MISS ANNA CHADWICK, who has achieved distinction in her line of work. She has high ideals in her story telling to children of all ages and is a charming companion for boys and girls. Her stories are not read or recited but are delivered in a dramatic and intelligent manner which never fails to leave the intended impression upon the minds of the hearers. As a means of education, development of the imagination, conversational ability the art of story-telling is recognized as of great value. She stays for a week and the boys and girls will greatly enjoy the hour with her in the Hall of Philosophy.

The work opens Tuesday, August 10, and continues through the week with Fairy Tales, Nature Stories, Myths, Folk-tales, Fables, closing on Saturday with miscellaneous stories.

These two clips from the 1908 program provide a glimpse into the "goings on" in the Hall of Philosophy during that season.

Besides the lectures and the children's story time held each day, there was often a series of "readings" in the afternoon, from performers such as Mrs. W.E. Lewis. These "readers" were a popular part of the Chautauqua program; they read selected works, such as "A Christmas Carol", and sketches from Shakespeare's "As you Like It."

Mrs. W.E. Lewis, Reader

From Mountain Chautauqua Poster.

After the Chautauqua fever tapered off, the building was not used for several years in the late 1920s, and was opened up and used once again for an area music program in the summer of 1932. After further disuse, the Hall of Philosophy was torn down in August 1936.

Philosophy Hall Razed At Mountain Lake Park

From The Republican 8-06-1936

The stones from the foundation of the Hall of Philosophy are likely seen in front of the Carr Cottage today, where they form a stone wall. Sarah Haynes' Father, Chis Haynes, told her they came from the "Latin School" building. For a closeup view of the Adirondack structure in front of the Hall, see the photo in the chapter covering Chautauqua Assemblies.

Stone Wall, Carr Cottage.

Detail of Hall of Philosophy foundation.

The Book Store, Refreshment Stand, and the Ticket office. (near 6 on Map)

G Street, looking North. Refreshment Stand on left, Ticket office on right foreground. Bookstore, just past the ticket office on the right. **Only the ticket office remains.** The Bookstore was an important outlet, selling supplies and books of the C.L.S.C. curriculum.

Refreshment Stand in the grove, ca. 1905. Sign in the front reads "Ice Cream". Tabernacle in the Background

Ticket Office Under Construction, Spring 1900.

The ticket office served as the entryway to the fenced amphitheater grounds. For the first 40 years of its existence, the center of the office had a dirt floor. It still stands today. The Amphitheater, under construction, looms in the background in the photo above. In the 1940s through the 1960s it served as a community meeting room, with groups like the Boy Scouts meeting there. Today it is the Museum for the Mt Lake Park Historical Association.

> The new ticket office at the entrance to the auditorium grounds is completed. It is an attractive building, differing in architecture from any other building in the Park. It is 42 x 32 feet, has a ticket office in the south end and a reception hall in the north end. The entrance to the grounds is between these two rooms. The

From the Republican, May 17, 1900 Edition

Ticket office 100 years later, ca. 2000.
Photo Courtesy of Karen Wooddell

Mt. Lake Bookstore on Left, Ticket Office on Right. Photo is from a glass negative of the W.E. Shirer Collection

William H. Malette operated the refreshment stand and bookstore for a few years around 1910. Occasionally, Mr. Malette ran into issues with the Association; once for selling postcards from his "porch." The contract to sell postcards had been assigned to the Terra Alta Candy Co.[9]

Another view of the Refreshment Stand, this with more signage, about 1905. Courtesy of Martha Kahl.

Association Buildings

In the early 1940s, Mrs. Nettie Eichlegerger bought the structure that was either the Book Store or the Refreshment stand and enclosed it. She moved her pie shop, which was located in the Chautauqua/Hotel England over to the building. Her pie shop was then named the **Sweet Shoppe**.[10] In the early 1950s, the **Gregory**'s operated the Mt. Lake Restaurant there. This building later became **El Lobos** in the late 1960s.

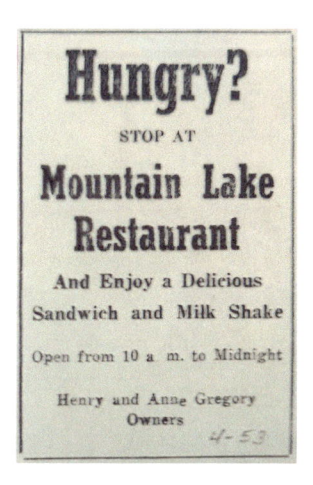

Gregory's ca. 1953, courtesy of Ed Poling.

Advert Gregory's 1953

El Lobo's Restaurant, near where the Bookstore was located after 1900. Torn down in 2001, it was earlier Gregory's. Restaurant. The Small white house on the far right is still standing as of 2022. Courtesy of Martha Kahl.

The Bashford Amphitheater (6 on Map)

The Bashford Amphitheater was built in 1900 and represents the pinnacle of activity in the Park. In the 1880s and 1890s, the crowds and interest in the Mountain Chautauqua had steadily grown; multiple expansions to the Tabernacle and the construction of the Hall of Philosophy could not contain the summer visitors.

Colorized Post Card View of the Amphitheater, Courtesy of Bob Boal.

Although the Ticket office and the Amphitheater were fenced, not everyone entered through the Ticket office doors:

"Several of us (children) used a hole in the fence by a large oak tree on the far side of the Auditorium fence instead of the gate. We could then spend our 15 cents at Malette's refreshment stand across the street"- **Ed C. Lewis, Born 1896.**[11]

Ed C. Lewis in 1916. Oakland High School Photo courtesy of Garrett County Historical Society

Amphitheater under construction, 1900. From W.E. Shirer Collection.

The Amphitheater (Amp) measured 172 feet in diameter and could accommodate up to 5000 people. The Architect was Mr. J.H. Cilley. from Lebanon County, Pa. Mr. Cilley had built at least two other smaller Amp's in Mt Gretna, Pa.[12] Building the Mt. Lake Amp, with its unique design, including the lack of interior supports, was a challenge for the carpenters assigned to the task. Robert Browning Garrett tells the following story, published in a 1956 edition of Tableland trails.

Tabernacle in Mt. Gretna, Pa. Also built by J.H. Cilley This Amp still stands.

William Sisk was a carpenter in and around Deer Park for many years. Bill really preferred fishing to working at his trade, being an easygoing bachelor. However, when ordinary carpenters were stumped by some intricate problem, Bill was hunted up for consultation. When the imposing summer home of the late James Swan Frick was being built by the Baltimore contracting firm of Philip Walsh and Sons, in 1892-93, the experienced carpenters from Baltimore had difficulty in laying out the ornamental staircase. Bill, then a young man, volunteered to show them how to do the job—and did so. A few years later, work on the amphitheater at Mountain Lake Park, with its unique system of roof supports, came to a standstill as the carpenters pondered over the complicated blue prints.

John H. Cilley From Findagrave.org

Someone, happily, remembered Bill Sisk, and was able to locate him. Bill soon cleared up the difficulty with the result that the graceful building that for many years was the pride of the neighborhood was brought to completion. On still another occasion, so it is said, the Deer Park interlocking tower was being built. A technical problem arose and work ceased. Then someone saw Bill Sisk calmly fishing in the Little Yough nearby. Shortly thereafter Bill had solved the problem, work was proceeding again.

Amphitheater, ca. 1903, Looking East.

"When you would sit down and look up at the ceiling of the amphitheater, it was just like looking at a big spider's web." **Mary Love**, recalled in 1980.

Mary Love, about the time she saw the Amp. for the first time.[13]

Amp., Band Playing, ca. 1903 Horses heading North on G Street. Courtesy of Keven Callis

Interior View of the Amphitheater, Mrs. Robert M. La Follett campaigning for her husband of the LaFollett-Wheeler Progressive Party Presidential Campaign, September, 1924. The Oakland band is on stage, left. Retrieved from Library of Congress.[14]

The La Follett campaign event caused a bit of a stir because it was held on a Sunday, and the topics were decidedly progressive and not religious.[15] Mrs. La Follett appealed directly to the women in the audience, *"It is women who must save and sacrifice to make the depreciated dollar cover the increased cost of living,"* said Mrs. La Follette. The times were changing in Mt. Lake Park.

"As a child, I can remember sitting on my mother's lap as we were driven in a black lacquered carriage out the dusty road to the Amphitheater where we heard the nation's foremost orators; and at the conclusion of their dramatic speeches (we) gave them a Chautauqua salute."- **E.R. O'Donnell, born 1882.**

The "Chautauqua Salute" is the tradition of waving one's handkerchief as a way of cheering, in lieu of clapping.

Association Buildings

Amphitheater—Seating Capacity 5,000, Mt. Lake Park, Md.

Amphitheater, Looking North, ca. 1930s. Bookstore on Left. Courtesy of Martha Kahl

> Mr. Cilley has completed the improvement to the Auditorium, and now there can be no question as to the absolute safety of the building.

From the Republican, 7-30-1908 edition

As the Mountain Chautauqua Assembly faded from view, fewer and fewer events we held in the Amp. Martha Kahl remembers going there to see the radio performers, "Jack and Flip", in the 1930s.

Like many of the other Association buildings in the 1930s and 1940s, the Amphitheater fell into disuse and was in need of repair. An estimate for the cost of repairs in 1940 was $9000. This was more than the $7500 it cost to build it originally. With this projected cost, combined with the fear of fire, a decision was made to tear down the Amphitheatre.

Apparently, there was some concern about the stability of the Amphitheater in 1908.

Amphitheatre during demolition, 1946

From <u>Once upon a Mountaintop</u>.

The Bowling Alley and Tennis Courts (7 on map)

(In the 30s) "My first job was as the librarian at the Bowling Alley" Mary I. Love, 1980.

The Bowling Alley and Tennis Courts were built in 1906, by a corporation formed by the Women's Civic Club. In 1906, one of the civic club's goals was to build a swimming pool. Building schedules were announced, but for unknown reasons, the pool never came to pass. The club did build a bowling alley and tennis courts, and at some point, ping pong tables were added. Bob Moore of Deer Park remembers "chasing the balls around", playing ping pong and bowling there. A few of the active members in the civic club were Mrs. Julia Walker Ruhl, Mrs. J. Summer Stone, and Mrs. John Thompson. Julia Ruhl and Mrs. Talson are among those credited with starting the library that was based in the building during the summer. The long running tennis tournaments are well chronicled in the Book "It's Tennis We Came to Play."

Pin and Balls from the Bowling Alley. These balls only have two holes in them.

Racquets from the Carr Cottage

INTERIOR OF BOWLING ALLEY.

Another activity at the Bowling Alley was the latest sensation, "Moving Pictures". Mr. Walker was showing movies at the Bowling Alley and the Amphitheater starting around 1910. Initially, there was grave concern that watching this new media could seriously damage one's eyesight.

In 1961 the Bowling alley was sold and dismantled;[16] the long alleyway was moved and used as two wings of a house up on Pittsburgh Ave. Today the building is the Town Hall. The wood walled interior is much as it was, and the bowling lanes are depicted in a mural.

11 - THE HOTELS AND BOARDING HOUSES

It is a bit unbelievable, the number of Hotels and Boarding Houses that have been in business in Mt. Lake. Reports are that, at one time, there were as many as 29 Hotels and Boarding houses in operation in the Park, *at the same time*. During the height of activity, roughly from 1894 through 1912, there were as many as 21,000 visitors to the park in a 10-week summer season.[1] While some of these people would make "day trips" on excursion trains, and later automobiles, many needed a place to stay. In fact, on the busiest events of the season, every room would be "fully booked" and folks would end up sleeping on porches and trying to stay awake at the train depot.

The business challenges to operating a hotel or boarding house for 10-12 weeks out of the year appear to be numerous. The effort to get it ready by mid-June, staff it and operate until the beginning of September, and then shut it down for nearly 8 months would cut into any potential profits. As we examine the history of these businesses, we can see that they changed hands numerous times and they were often under "new management." To add the other uncertainties, we can include the weather; if it was a rainy summer, the operators could watch their profits wash away. It appears that many were tempted by the lure of the crowds but few could make a long-term "go" of it.

We shall start with the Hotels and then transition to the Boarding Houses. Most of the Hotels are identified in the first map in the beginning of this book.

Hotels

When it comes to hotels, Jennie Smith's family had an outsized impact on the Park hotel and dining trade. Many of her extended family, including Jennie's mother, arrived in the Park in March of 1883;[2] they brought with them furniture, horses, and wagons. In addition to Jennie Smith operating the Grace Cottage, several other relatives were involved in the Park hospitality:

- **Adam Howell**, Jennie's Brother-in-law, along with Jennie's sister **Fannie**, operated the dining hall at Grace Cottage and built the Columbian Hotel. He later operated the Allegheny House.

- **James O. Smith**, Jennie's Brother, had a baggage and hack business and with his wife, **Dora E. (Sandy) Smith** operated Mt. Washington Inn at the corner of Philadelphia and K street.

- **Mrs. Daniel Smith** (Jennie's Sister-in-law) and her husband, Jennie's brother, built and operated the Braethorn Inn/Hotel

Although the Smith's built and operated several of the large hotels and boarding houses and were well regarded, they most often appeared to incur financial loses, which ultimately caused them to sell or lose their businesses.

Next, we will cover the hotels in semi-chronological order.

Mt. Lake Hotel

We have already covered the Mt. Lake Hotel, in the chapter under Association Buildings. As noted, that hotel was the first to come and the last to go. Some of the owners included Mr. Van Meter, Mr. L.T. Yoder, Mr. Dunnington (June's Father), June Dunnington Grimes (Martha Grimes' mother) and Mrs. William H. Davis. Mrs. Grimes and Mrs. Davis also operated the Pickwick Inn in Oakland, Maryland.

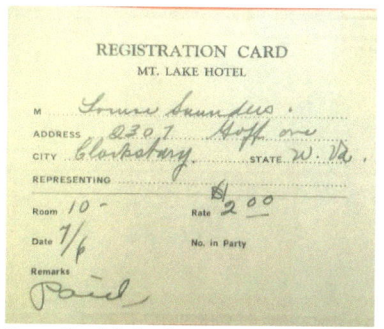

Reg. Card July 6, year unknown. We could not locate info on Laura Saunders from Clarksburg.

Mt. Lake Hotel Porch, ca. 1910

The sparsely appointed hotel lobby, from the 1895 Mountain Chautauqua. This photo differs from the earlier photo in the Association Buildings Chapter. As the hotel was dismantled, two sections of the front desk were reclaimed; one is in the Ticket Office Museum and the other is in Carr Cottage. Note the suspended lamps in this photo.

101

Mt. Lake Hotel ca. 1895. From Cumberland County Museum, A.A. Line Collection

Grace Cottage / Chautauqua Hotel / Thoburn Inn / Hotel England

"It was now time to prepare for the summer's work. I gave all the year to evangelistic work except two or three months in the summer when I rested by keeping boarders. I enjoyed home work. As a rule I had students and others who needed the mountain air and were self supporting as my help in this. During the season various gatherings come to this resort. The camp meeting was one of great interest. All denominations took part, it was almost a national meeting." **Miss Jennie Smith, describing Grace Cottage in the 1880s.**[3]

Grace Cottage.

MISS JENNIE SMITH, Superintendent of the Railroad Department of the Women's Christian Temperance Union, will have her Cottage ready for her friends by the first of June. A lovely home for Christian Workers, and a Christian home for all. She may be addressed at MOUNTAIN LAKE PARK, Garrett Co., Md.

From Mt. Lake Messenger, 1884

From B&O magazine Vol 2, No.3 1913

EVANGELIST JENNIE SMITH

GRACE COTTAGE, MOUNTAIN LAKE PARK, MD., HOME OF JENNIE SMITH.

From Jennie Smith's 1887 book, <u>Ramblings in Beula Land</u>.

Mountain Lake Park
CENTRAL DINING ROOMS,
(Connected with Miss Jennie Smith's Cottage.)

A. HOWELL, Proprietor.

Conveniently Located close to the Camp Enclosure.
MEALS $1.00 per DAY. Breakfast and Supper 35cts. each. Dinner 50cts.
Meals served at all hours. Lodgings for Gentlemen, above Dining Rooms, at reasonable rates.

From Mt. Lake Messenger, 1884.

Adam Howell would go on to own, then lose, the Columbian Hotel, and then manage the Allegheny House.

Dinner for 400 – "80 Chickens, 2 Sheep, 50 Pounds of Beef, and 14 Hams"…

We see from the Advertisement, above, that Jennie Smith's Brother-in-law, Adam Howell, along with Jennie's sister Fannie, ran the "Central Dining Rooms" that were located just behind Grace Cottage. What follows is an 1887 account by Jennie Smith about feeding 400 people for dinner and 300 for supper

Jennie Smith's description of dinner for 400, written in her breezy style.

A RAILROAD GATHERING We often had excursions I worked up one I knew I would have to feed at least one hundred so I laid in a good supply and made arrangements with the butchers bakers etc so I could call on them if needed That morning I called my help together after prayer I said Now we must stand on the promise today AS THY DAY SO SHALL THY STRENGTH BE I gave all their orders A half hour afterwards a telegram Four hundred at Grace Hotel for dinner I read it to the cook saying Aunt Julia what do you think of this She replied "Well the Lord will just have to make His promise good and we will trust Him to do it."

We fed four hundred for dinner and three hundred for supper could seat two hundred at once in the dining room. I advertised dinners for twenty five cents. We could hardly believe the amount that was consumed <u>eighty chickens two sheep fifty pounds of beef fourteen hams</u> and everything else in accord. All went like clockwork with nineteen helpers besides Mrs Miller and girls Mrs Sheets and girls helped wait on table It was fun for them I entertained thirty five band boys and the speakers. We had a great meeting a memorable day.

As described in an earlier chapter, Jennie eventually fell ill and lost the Hotel, it was renamed Chautauqua Hotel. Jennie's Brother, Daniel Smith (who would later operate the Braethorn) continued helping in the operations of the Hotel Chautauqua after Jennie lost control of the venture.[4]

From 1898 Edition of Mt. Chautauqua.

The Hotels and Boarding Houses

From her last book, ca. 1920 Jennie Smith died in 1924

Approaching Hotel Chautauqua from Arbutus Drive. Braethorn in left background

Mr. and Mrs. T.D. Richards bought the Hotel Chautauqua in 1898; they lived in the Chautauqua Cottage just behind the hotel. That cottage still stands today.

The name of the Hotel was changed to the Thoburn Inn in 1920, and a new "cafeteria" was installed.

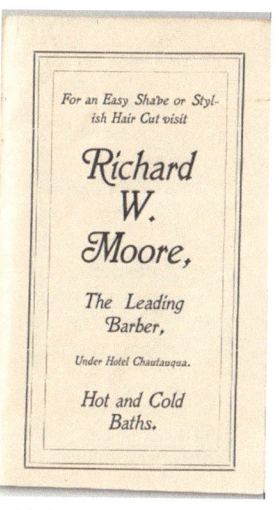

For an Easy Shave or Stylish Hair Cut visit

Richard W. Moore,

The Leading Barber,

Under Hotel Chautauqua.

Hot and Cold Baths.

Richard Moore, a Black man, was a barber; he operated his business in the Chautauqua Hotel and other locations.

Postcard shows walking path from the Grove to Thoburn. The way it was before the construction of State Route 135.

The Braethorn and Thoburn   Mountain Lake Park, Maryland

Postcard View from the Grove

After 1920, Mr. Howard W. Hamilton, of Pittsburgh, was the manager of the cafeteria and the Inn.

In 1940 Mr. and Mrs C.A. Wetzel, took charge of the Thoburn, with the plan to operate it as a "modern hotel."[5]

In July of 1940, the hotel was renamed "Hotel England" Named in honor of the Miss Ocie England, then head of the Park owners group.[6]

In 1942, Miss Nettie Eichleberger was operating a pie shop in the hotel. The Hotel disappears, (torn down?) sometime between 1942 and 1955.

Faith Home/Hamilton Hall

"Faith Home was another Hotel. (It was) run by a lady from Virginia who paid kids for raking her grounds with a bag of raw peanuts." **Recalling his childhood, Ed C. Lewis, born 1896.**

Faith Home was built around 1888, by Sarah Harris, a member of the Women's Temperance Christian Union (W.T.C.U.) It was leased to Jennie Smith for her "home" in 1894. It is not clear when Faith Home name was changed to Hamilton Hall, but by the summer of 1921, Mrs. Belle Kisner, and Mrs. Clyde Liller take charge of Hamilton Hall.[7] In 1941 the Hotel was purchased by Dr. Mutchler, of Florida., a leader of an Accordion band.[8] Hamilton Hall was later used for student residences for the short-lived 'Self-help' University.

We can think of a new Advertising tag line:

"Faith Home, where kids will literally work for peanuts."

Sarah C. Harris, Owner of Faith Home, from Franklin, Va.[9]

Hamilton Hall was sold at auction in 1963 and torn down in the mid-1960's.

Dennett/Overlook Hotel

The Dennett Hotel was located at the corner of what is now called Dennett Road and Deer Park Ave. It was built in 1890 by Mr. Alfred W. Dennett, an owner of a "quick lunch" restaurant chain and hotels in New York, Philadelphia and Baltimore.[10]

Mr. Dennett was an unusual man; he earned vast wealth through his restaurants and hotels while at the same time, he was an over-zealous religious crusader.[11]

In his restaurants, Mr. Dennett posted religious signs admonishing customers to find their way towards his religion, or else. For his waitresses he posted signs, such as

"Be ye strong, therefore, and let not your hands be weak, for your work shall be rewarded." He required his employees to pray on schedule during their shifts, they would be fined if they missed a prayer session. Because of the fines, his employees rarely took home a full paycheck. And, yes, his restaurants were closed on Sundays.

He was a strong backer of temperance and he even went so far as to help organize citizen-vice squads; he conducted surveillance, looking into businesses suspected of 'immoral' activities.[12] Needless to say, Mr. Dennett became deeply interested in Mt. Lake Park. He arrived on the scene in 1889. The December 14, 1889 edition of the Republican picks up the story:

1896 Mt. Chautauqua

Mr. A. W. Dennett arrived here last Wednesday evening and brought one of his daughters with him to attend Miss Swan's school. He awarded the contract of his building to Mr. A. C. Brooke, of Oakland. The building is to be 37x100, two-stories, with a veranda along the entire south side, which takes in the finest view of the mountains of any place on — the grounds. Mr. Dennett's special object is to provide a home for ministers and evangelists who cannot afford to pay such high prices for accommodations after they get here, the men are now burning off the brush on the building site so that the foundation can be put in this winter if the weather will permit.

A few years later, in 1896, Mrs. E.E. Williams describes an addition of the Dennett Hotel: *"a large reception hall, beatifically furnished, leading into a chapel of Magnificent proportions, seated with chairs for religious services. Above there are bedrooms of great beauty and convenience, crowned at the summit by an observatory, from which a most commanding view can be obtained."*[13]

The 75 room Dennett / Overlook Hotel

The Hotels and Boarding Houses

Away from the smoke of the R. R.

Excellent Baths.

Sanitary Plumbing.

Lighted by Gas.

Superior Cuisine by Experienced Chef.

Free Bus.

Hotel Dennett Advertisement. Note that it leads with "Away from the smoke of the Railroad" Folks likely had to contend with a great deal of soot and cinders closer to the tracks. Hotel Dennett was quite far from the 'action' at the Tabernacle and Amphitheatre, hence the "free bus".
From the Mountain Chautauqua

Spoons from the Hotel Dennett.
Courtesy of Bob Boal.

Mr. Alfred W. Dennett Retrieved from findagrave.org

Rare Interior View of Dennett/Overlook Hotel

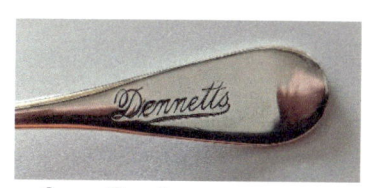

Advertisement for Dennett's Restaurant in Philadelphia

Spoon Detail

In the mid-1890s, Mr. Dennett began investing in mining companies in California. He was already a millionaire but he wanted to make more money, pledging to donate his earnings to charity and religious endeavors. These investments and others did not go well. In the late 1890s, Mr. Dennett lost all of his money and suffered a series of mental breakdowns. He was eventually institutionalized in California.

And so, in 1901, the Dennett Hotel was sold, and renamed the Overlook Hotel. By the summer of 1902, Mrs. Lillian Blanche Creel (L.B.C.) List was placed in charge of the Overlook Hotel. Mrs List had been operating the stylish Loch Lynn Heights Hotel. That hotel was "across the tracks" and had a grand ballroom with Saturday night dances, a casino, and other forbidden "amusements".

From the Clarksburg Telegram 6-16-1902

Loch Lynn Hotel W.Blair Simmons told his daughter, Carolyn Corley, this was Mrs. L.B.C. List, operator of this hotel and the Overlook Inn.

After a couple of years, Mrs. List returned to the Loch Lynn Hotel and the Overlook ran into financial disputes and was abandoned. It appears that it was closed for good around 1905. An out-of-town reporter, from the Carroll Record newspaper, provided this saddening description of touring the deserted Overlook in 1909:

> *We will close this letter with a single odd experience— that'of going through a deserted, or unused, fully furnished hotel of 75 rooms —Overlook Inn. A hotel which has been the victim of financial trouble and consequent litigation, mixed with personal stubbornness, for the past four or five years. Through a friend, we secured the key of the building and went through it from top to bottom; The interior, as well as exterior, is going to ruins. Leaking roofs and dampness have played havoc with walls and furniture and very good furniture too.*
>
> *The dining-room tables, stacked with queensware, glassware and table linen. The bedrooms are furnished, except as to carpets and linen; mattresses—all of them excellent quality felt the blankets and comforters are more or less in confusion, but there; the oak furniture is swollen and warped, the nicely up holstered parlor furniture is practically ruined; the office paraphernalia, everything about the place, will soon be worthless junk, and one can't help but ask the question, time and again, whether there is any sensible reason for such a condition.*
>
> *The whole muddle 'seems to rest on two overlapping mortgages, and contrariness, and this is the condition of a beautifully located house, at which we had the unwelcome experience, five years ago, of being turned away because there was "no room at the Inn," We were glad to get out again, for the house seemed to have a lot of dead people in it some where.*

In 1918, the building was sold and torn down. The advert below is from the June 19, 1919 edition of the Republican newspaper.

For Sale at Half Price at Mt. Lake Park
by
A. A. and T. D. RICHARDS

All the building material lately in the Hotel Dennett. Some of the finest lumber to be found anywhere, from plastering lath up to timbers 40 feet long and of every description. Furniture, including office counter, windows and doors, trimmed complete; large hotel range, 100 gallon boiler, 500 bbl. tank and tower, water and gas iron pipe; soil and sewer pipe; bath tubs, building stone, brick, etc.

We have also 21½ Lots, well shaded, and adjoining these, 4¾ Acres of fine land under cultivation, and by combining these we will sell villa sites as desired, with gardens and truck lots attached. Call on or phone
T. D. RICHARD,
Chautauqua Cottage, Mt. Lake Park.

June 19, 1919 Advert. Republican

One wonders where all the Hotel Dennett materials ended up. They are likely in many of the Mt. Lake and Oakland homes today. Also, from this advert, we can see that Mr. T.D. Richards had a store and lived in the Chautauqua Cottage. Mary Love found a diary of Mrs. Richards from the year of 1911 and based her book upon that diary. Alas, that diary has not been recovered.

Dr. and Mrs. T.D. Richards in 1936.

Footnote: another surprising episode that Mr. Dennett was involved in was the "Lincoln boyhood farm" and the so-called "Lincoln and Davis" cabins. A brief summary: Mr. Dennett bought the Lincoln Farm, Sinking Springs, in Kentucky, but then found out there was no cabin on it. His aim was to create a tourist attraction. He had a cabin moved from a neighboring farm, named it the "Lincoln Cabin" and set up business. The tourist business was not good (the location was remote), so he moved the cabin to Nashville. There he also brought the "Davis Cabin" thought to belong to Jefferson Davis. After a Nashville exhibit, his crew started moving the cabins from town to town. After a few moves, the crew got the logs mixed up, so they just built one big cabin and named it the "Lincoln-Davis Cabin". Mr. Dennett went bankrupt, the cabins were sold to a creditor and eventually they ended up back at Sinking Springs Farm, which is now managed by the National Parks Service. A cabin made of some of the logs is still on display there now. The NPS has carbon-dated the logs and they date to 1849, well after either Lincoln or Davis were boys. Much more info on this subject can be obtained if the reader searches the Internet.

Oak Hall

Photo Courtesy of Bob Boal

Another Park hotel was, "Oak Hall", built in 1892 by Mr. and Mrs. Thaddens Hinebaugh.[14] The Hinebaughs also operated the Randolph hotel in Elkins, WV. Oak Hall was located across from the Tabernacle, between D and E streets, what would now be just at the entrance of Baltimore Ave and near St. Rte. 135. The hill has been called "Oak Hall hill". The Hinebaughs operated Oak Hall for a number of years, then used it as the summer residence.

Note the different spelling of Mrs. (Minnie Phillips) Himbaugh's name in the advertisement. There are a few different spellings.

A.B. Fleming, the former Governor of West Virginia purchased Oak Hall for his summer residence in 1902.[15] The Flemings spent their summers there at least through 1906. It is not clear how long the building stood after 1906, it is said to have ultimately burnt down.

Gov. Aretas B. Fleming and wife, Carrie W. Fleming. Courtesy WV History on View

Advert from 1895 Mt. Chautauqua.

The Oak Hall architect, W.A. Liller was a prominent builder of Cottages and Hotels in Mt. Lake. He also built the first pump house for the "water works" in Mt. Lake Park.[16]

W.A. Liller

Columbian Hotel

The Columbian was a large hotel built in 1893 by Mr. Adam Howell.[17] He was married to Jennie Smith's sister, Fannie, and they operated the dining hall at the Hotel Chautauqua. The Columbian was located on Deer Park Avenue; near the corner of Oakland Drive and Deer Park Ave. The Hotel seemed to be a bit ill-fated, as there were accidents, bankruptcies, and a sudden death all within the first few years.

- In July, 1893, Mr. Howell was injured while unloading a wagon He nearly died but he did eventually recover.[18]
- By 1896, Mr. Howell had lost the Mortgage on the Hotel, it was sold and he leased the Allegheny house, to operate for the season.
- In 1899, Perry Spiker, whom had leased the Columbian died suddenly.[19]

Shortly after that, things seemed to stabilize at the Columbian. The Hanson B. Lewis family purchased and operated the hotel. Mr. Lewis's wife, Barbara Ann (Weimer) Lewis was a first cousin to Miss Josie Weimer, whose family built the Colonial Boarding house in 1903.

Recalls the Lewis' son, **Ed**:

"Father had his own icehouse after he bought the Columbian. He also erected a tank on a 60 foot tower between the stable and the hotel with a gasoline engine and furnished water for them and the Braethorn."

Like many locals, World War I took Ed out of the area and he only occasionally returned. *"I joined the Marines at the outbreak of World War I and I never went back except for a short visit".*

Columbian Hotel, Mountain Lake Park, Md.

COLUMBIAN HOTEL. Centrally Located, Near Auditorium.
Is re-opened and newly furnished, and will be ready for guests June 15. From $6 to $10 per week. For further particulars, address JOHN SHARTZER, Mt. Lake Park, Garrett Co., Md.

Even before the World War disrupted business in the United States, the big hotels were showing signs of distress. In March of 1914, the Columbian was purchased by Dr. Charles Fazenbaker, who planned to tear down the Columbian and make a cottage out of some of the material. It is not clear if Dr. Fazenbaker executed his plan, because in Jan. 1918, the following "For Sale" notice appeared in the Republican paper.

That concludes our section on the hotels; none remain, but in their heyday, they hosted thousands of visitors, musicians, lecturers, and teachers. They employed hundreds of people, and drove demand for farmers' crops from miles around.

FOR SALE

Having purchased the large Columbian Hotel with all its contents at Mt Lake, will be there daily and offer at private sale the following:

A large lot of bedsteads, mattresses, springs, dressers, washstands, chairs, tables, doors and windows with frames, lath, bricks, etc. and all kinds of lumber for buildings.

The above will be sold at greatly reduced prices.

The Mt. Lake Park Wrecking Co.
Box No. 264.   Oakland, Md.
J. S. Gnegy, Secretary.

The Boarding Houses

To kick off this section, it is useful to draw a distinction between a boarding house and a hotel. While we are all familiar with a hotel and the process of making reservations and staying, a boarding house is a bit more antiquated operation and may require some definition.

The difference between Mt. Lake boarding houses and hotels starts with the scale of the operation. As we reviewed the Park's hotels, many of them could accommodate up to 200 guests. The largest boarding houses, on the other hand, could house up to 30 or 40 guests, with many smaller ones having just a few lodging rooms. Another substantial difference is the dining experience. The big hotels like the Mt. Lake Hotel and the Grace Cottage (Hotel) had large dining halls that could feed hundreds of diners. The boarding houses had relatively small dining rooms, that might serve up to 20 boarders at a time. At the boarding houses, meals were laid out at a set time, such as 8am, 1pm and 6pm, and served "family style"; at the big hotels folks were seated in waves and plated meals were brought to their table.

Several boarding houses were family-operated. Miss Josie Weimer remembers: *"One summer we had as many as 36 boarders and about 20 of them stayed in"*. (Meaning the other boarders just came for meals.) *"We all worked together but mother supervised.""*

Many of the cottages in the Park switched between smaller boarding houses and private cottages, depending upon the owner of the day. For this section, we will just focus on the larger boarding houses that were ongoing "businesses".

Allegheny House

The Allegheny House, located on H street, was the earliest boarding house built and one of the longest running. Construction was completed in June of 1882, and the first guests arrived at the beginning of July.[20]

Lorilla Bullard built the boarding house; she owned and operated it for more than 20 years. Lorilla was married to George R. Bullard. The Allegheny was large as boarding houses go, with 13 bedrooms.

Allegheny House, early 1900s. Courtesy of Walter Pollard, Jr.

Advert 1884 Mt. Lake Messenger Note the different spelling.

The Allegheny was a popular lodging place for groups. In particular, the youths from the Epworth League would stay at both the Allegheny and the Colonial, which was right behind the Allegheny. The girls would stay in one boarding house and the boys would stay in the other. They would then sing hymns (acceptable songs at the time) back and forth through the night; we can imagine what other mischief they might get up to.

Said to be a portrait of **Mrs. Bullard**. This still hangs in the Allegheny House.

The Allegheny sports a "built-in" Ice Box. Courtesy of Walter Pollard, Jr.

Eastlake Settee, Original to the Allegheny.

Original Gas Stove, Courtesy of Walter Pollard, Jr.

Thought to be Mrs. Bullard or her daughter.

Mrs. Bullard's daughter and son, Lorilla F. Bullard, and Thur Emil Bullard, were both doctors. Mrs. Bullard passed away in 1912.

According to the Republican newspaper, in 1902, L.A. Rusdisill and W.L Davidson purchased the Allegheny:

> The Allegany House has been purchased by Messrs. Rudisill and Davidson. It will be thoroughly overhauled and newly furnished next season. A new roof will be put on this fall.

These "insiders" must have seen the value of the boarding house.

Around 1915, Maj.. William N., and Mina F. Skyles purchased the Allegheny house. The Skyles were very active in the Western Maryland Tennis Championships, as described in the book, It's Tennis We Came to Play. It was operated as a boarding house until the 1930s and has remained in the Skyles/Pollard family for more than 100 years.

Maj. William F. and Mina F. Sklyes, Courtesy of Walter Pollard, Jr.

Thompson Rest Home For Deaconesses and "The Annex"

"We came first in the summer of 1882. The cottage was only partly completed and we have always loved to recall those days of 'roughing' it." **Mrs. Mary Thompson, 1916**

Rev. John Thompson Deaconess Home

Burlington on right, also known as the "Annex".

The Thompson Rest Home was built in 1882, by Rev. John Thompson and his wife. The initial structure was built as a summer home for the Thompsons, that they might have their own place to stay and entertain during the camp meetings. As mentioned elsewhere, the Thompson's were some of the earliest summer residents and were pillars of the camp meeting experience.

Just before she died in 1916, Mrs. Thompson recalled the early days of building up the Park:[21]

It seems hardly possible that almost four decades have passed since Mr. Thompson and I, with our little family, first saw the outline of these mountains which grew to be so unspeakably dear to us. We came first in the summer of 1882. This cottage was then only partly completed and we have always loved to recall those days of "roughing it,"—our nearest approach to pioneering,—when we, like the old Gideonites, were literally "hewers of wood and drawers of water," for there were fences to build, wood-sheds to fill, stumps to be uprooted, stones to be gathered and taken away, and every drop of water to be carried from the old auditorium grounds, where we had, that first summer, a common well.

And there may be a few here today who will recall some humorous battles with over friendly snakes and an unesthetic animal who wished to dwell with us on too hospitable terms. There was plenty of hard work but there were also days in the woods, with well-filled baskets and happy talk and song, and there was the still more blessed Sabbaths when we met for prayer.

Rev. John and Mary Thompson

In 1899, in failing health, Bishop Thompson sold the home to the Women's Home Missionary Society, Mrs. Rudisill was one of the founders of this group; they operated it as a Rest Home for Deaconesses.

The "Annex"

The "Annex" was initially known as the "Burlington", it was located in the lots next to the Thompson home; it started as a standalone structure, built in 1900 by Miss Orum, the teacher of Elocution in the Park. The "Annex" cottage was shortly thereafter sold to Rev. Fallon, husband of the late Maggie Watson and owner of the Maggie Watson cottage, located just across the street. For a number of years, the Maggie Watson/Fallon Cottage and the Burlington/Annex were operated as a combined boarding business, by Mrs. Blue. Ultimately, in 1917, the Annex and the Deaconess were connected and used as the rest home. In a 1951 article, Jared Young describes the evolution of the Thompson cottage to the Deaconess, to include the Annex:

THE BURLINGTON will be opened for the entertainment of guests July first. Best located and most popular boarding house in the Park. Until June first address Mrs S. E. Blue, Homer, Ohio; after that date Mt. Lake Park, Maryland.

Advert ca. 1903

> About the Century's turn, a group of Park women, deeply interested in a branch of Church work then known as the Woman's Home Missionary Society, began a project of their own along general Association lines. This was a summer home where hard working Church Deaconesses could enjoy a vacation at a cost commensurate with their meager wage. The women formed a corporation, The Thompson Rest Home of Garrett County, Md.; and bought "Bishop" Thompson's former residence with its three lots. To operate the Home they secured the efficient services of a Deaconess, Miss Octavia Hicks, who continued in the work for upward of forty years. Later, as its needs increased the old Sharp residence on two lots adjoining the Home was acquired, and named the Annex.
>
> ...(from Jared Young, 1951)

There was also a large dining hall at the Deaconess, operated in later years by Mrs. Ethel Turney. *"Miss (Octavia) Hicks had it for many years and then (later) I started cooking for the camp meeting,"* **Mrs. Turney recalled**.[22] In the 1930s and 1940s, the Deaconess housed a School of Missions and a girls camp during the summers.

The Annex was torn down around 2009; the Deaconess still stands in 2023.

Another specialized boarding house was the **Briarbend Seminary**, built in 1884, which was actually a boarding school for girls and boys. The school appears to have started in 1887. One of the advert tag lines was *"No Liquor, No City Temptations, No Malaria"*. The school was operated by Miss E.B. Swan, originally from Milwaukee. WI. In 1931, Briarbend was taken down and the lumber was used to build a club house at Deep Creek Lake, in Green Glade.

Briarbend Seminary, from 1893 Mt. Chautauqua.

Relocated Briarbend, 2022.

Braethorn

The Braethorn, at the corner of G street and Arbutus Drive (now Route. 135), was built on or before 1896 by Mrs. Daniel Smith, the sister-in-law of Jennie Smith. The building received a two-story addition in the spring of 1897[23]. The Braethorn had a long run as a boarding house and was later converted to an apartment complex for a number of years.

In December 1901, Mrs. Smith sold the Braethorn to Mrs. Josiah Lockhart Campbell for $2,250.[24] Mrs. Campbell's given and maiden name was Gertrude Baxter. Dr. Josiah Campbell was a Surgeon and Captain in the 10th Virginia Infantry in the Civil War.

"BRAETHORN," MT. LAKE PARK, MD.

Braethorn, Postcard Courtesy of Bob Boal

Mrs. Campbell evidently knew what she was doing when it came to running an Inn, as she received warm reviews and operated the Braethorn for more than 30 years.

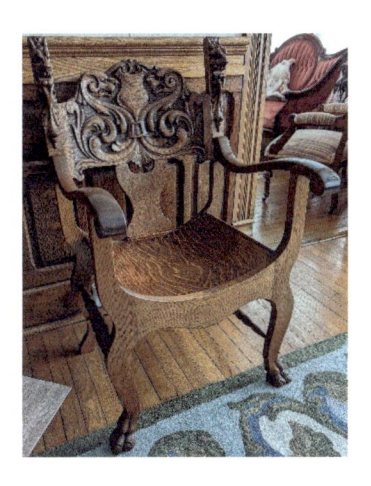

Ornate Chair from the lobby of the Braethorn. Courtesy of Karen Wooddell.

Braethorn

One of the Most Conveniently Located Houses at Mt. Lake Park with all modern improvements.

Conducted on the Old Virginia Style

For Terms Address,
MRS. J. L. CAMPBELL,
WINCHESTER, VA.
After June 5, MT. LAKE PARK, MD.

Advert ca. 1910

Braethorn at the end of the line, ca 1980 Photo by Mary Love

The second and third stories were described as having long hallways, with small, sparsely furnished rooms, and, in later years, a bath at each end of the halls. The Braethorn was one of a few Park buildings that featured a French-style mansard roof. The flat roof survived many snowy seasons in the Park. In the late 1930s, Mrs. Campbell's daughter, Gertrude (Campbell) Thraves continued to operate the Braethorn after her mother's passing. The Braethorn had a large dining hall and continued to host dinners and community events through the 1940s. By the late 1940s, the Braethorn made a slow transition to apartments.

The Braethorn stood until 1988, when, despite some discussions to restore it, the old inn was torn down.

Photo from the Jan. 21, 1988 edition of The Republican.

The Colonial

Edwin Arthur and brother Charles Weimer built the Colonial in 1903, for their mother, Martha Friend Weimer, so that she might operate a boarding house. Martha Weimer and her husband, Joseph Weimer, had lived near Friendsville, where Joseph was a farmer. Joseph died suddenly and this instigated the migration of Martha and her five Weimer children to Mt. Lake Park. Nearly all of the Weimer children eventually became school teachers, and Edwin would go on to operate a store in Oakland. Martha's three daughters were named Lillian, Cora, and Josie.

Lillian and Cora were local school teachers. At one time, Lillian taught at the Broadford school out on Kings Run Road; she "commuted" daily to school by walking from the Colonial, three miles each way.[25] In 1915, Cora was the Librarian at the Oakland Free Public Library.

Charles Weimer

Edwin A. Weimer

The Colonial has approximately 9 bedrooms and a large basement. The Weimers operated the house year-round, and they eventually took on several long-term boarders. As described in the chapter on Winter, the Weimer daughters, primarily Miss Josie and Cora, hosted the town library in winter.

Miss Josie recalls the Weimer family move to the Park.[26]

"We rented the Dixie cottage (this house, now gone, was near the North West corner of what is now G street and Rt. 135) the year before we built here. It was a rainy year in 1903 and the house didn't get finished when we thought it would, and we had already rented rooms, so we got rooms for one bunch of boarders at Capt. Hayden's house (across the street) and another bunch in what is now the Teagarden House. (The first) Boarders came when we had temporary steps and no banisters on the 2nd floor."

After her mother (Martha) died, Miss Josie and her sisters ran the Colonial for several decades.

The Colonial ca. 1910.

Martha, Josie and Lillian (or Cora) Weimer. *ca. 1909.*

In the Colonial, Josie Weimer on the right, and (thought to be) her cousin Sudie Friend on the Left. Courtesy of Kathy Malone.

Josie Weimer was a cook, so we could speculate on what she was doing with the hatchet. Courtesy of Kathy Malone.

The Colonial Dining Room, said to be a turkey dinner on the table.

On an audio recording from 1980, Mary Love tells a story about Jared Young, a long-time boarder at the Colonial. Apparently, Jared was a late sleeper, breakfast was served at 8:00am. After everyone gathered, with no sign of Jared, one of the other boarders would grab a pair of scissors off the bureau and bang on the pipes that went up through his room. That usually was enough to wake him up.

The Colonial has changed hands several times over the years; it seems new owners, such as Jim and Shirley Munford (now former owners), come along when needed and restore the property. It still stands today.

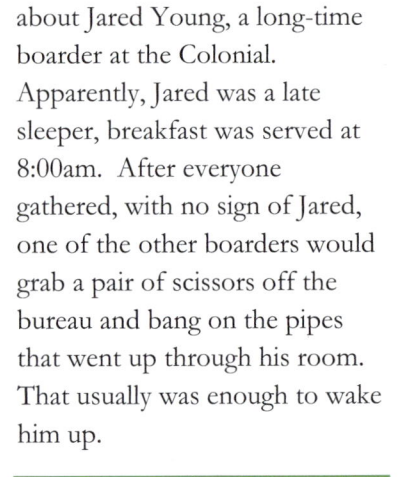

From the Colonial. Courtesy of Bob & Dixie Moore.

Mt. Washington Home

This boarding house was at the corner of K street and Philadelphia Ave., just south of the Mt. Lake Park School and just north of the Mt. Lake Hotel. This boarding house was built and furnished in the spring of 1898 by James O. Smith, brother of Jennie Smith, and his wife Emma Smith. Mrs. Smith operated the house for several years; later it became the Schrock Boarding house. Mrs. Schrock operated the house for nearly 30 years. Eventually the house was torn down.

> Mrs. J. O. Smith is furnishing the Mt. Washington House. She is go- to have a cozy place for "summer people."

From the Republican, March 25, 1898

MT. WASHINGTON HOME,
Situated Cor. K St. and Philadelphia Ave.
One of the Best Equipped Boarding Houses on the Park. Thoroughly Painted and Papered. Large Dining Room where a Generous Table is provided with all the Delicacies of the Season, under the personal supervision of the Proprietress, MRS. J. O. SMITH, who will attend to the care and comfort of her guests. Rates, $1.00 to $1.50 per Day. Special Rates for Camp-Meeting.
MRS. J. O. SMITH, Mt. Lake Park, Md.

Photo Courtesy of Martha Kahl.

Queenwood / Park View Lodge

A Missionary, a Magician, and an Escape Artist.

At one point in time, in August of 1911, the following guests were staying at Queenwood: Mrs. H. S. Jenanyan, widow of Dr. H. S. Jenanyan, the well-known Armenian missionary, accompanied by her daughter. Also staying were Mr. Dana Walden, the great magician, and the famous escape artist Heverly. We can only imagine their conversations on the porch.

These visitors, a missionary and an escape artist, can be thought of as the "bookends" of the Chautauqua movement in Mt. Lake; starting with the Camp Meetings and evolving towards the Vaudeville-type acts.

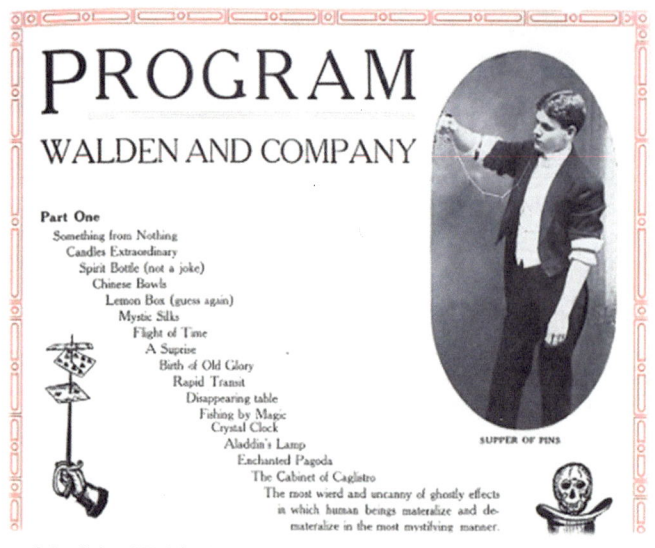

Magician Walden's program, retrieved from Univ. Iowa Libraries

Linden Heverly ca. 1920. He was also a 'mystic'.

In the early 1900s, George W. Clawson was the owner of the 26 room Queenwood and he leased it out to several individuals to operate. The amount of "churn" of folks leasing it point to either bad business conditions or some inherent problem at Queenwood:

In 1909, the Queenwood was leased and operated by B.F. Crane, of Loch Lynn. In 1911, the rooming house was leased by Catharine B. Ottley, of Grafton, WV. In 1913, Misses Fannie Schaffer and her sister leased the Queenwood. Evidently, this was not their "cup of tea" as there was a new operator, Miss Minnie Gull, by August in the same summer of 1913. In Oct. of 1913, Mr. H.E. Felty, of Felty's store (next door) leased the property and moved in with his family. By the early 1920s, the building had been vacant for a number of years.

In 1922, the building was remodeled and renamed Park View Lodge, operated by Mrs. Travers. Slowly, as the Park's summer business declined, the Park View became a year-round boarding house, with long-term tenants. In October of 1946, all the contents and the building were offered for sale. Eventually, it was converted to apartments and it still stands today.

Park View Lodge ca. 1930. Courtesy of Martha Kahl. Stanley Wood's (Martha's Father) Truck on Left.

Maryland Home

Maryland Home, on H street, was built by P.T. Garthright around 1896. Mr. Garthright was a merchant and builder and was active for many years in the Park. As seen in Mr. Garthright's postcard illustration, it was a big house, with a large additional wing for boarders.

In 1898, Mrs M.C. Reinhart was running the Maryland. She offered a "new and thoroughly painted" home, with a large dining room and a "generous table". Rates ranged from $1.00-$2.00 per day.

> Saturday about 11.00 a, m. some one entered the room of the help of the Maryland Home and opened the trunks and suit cases and stole all the money found in them, which consisted of the wagas paid them, a few days previous. The theif has not been discovered.

Despite efforts to the contrary, Maryland Home, like the rest of the Park, was not immune from petty thefts and other "immoral acts". From the Republican, 9-13-1914.

Maryland Home was the scene of more than one incident over the years: The headline from the Feb. 2, 1928 Republican read:

FEDERAL MEN GET STILL AT MT. LAKE ON TUESDAY

One of the most completely equipped and costly stills ever to be captured in Garrett County, according to Sheriff William D. Casteel, with 28 barrels of mash and 100 gallons of moonshine liquor, was that uncovered and destroyed by a Federal Prohibition officer assisted by Sheriff Casteel, at Mountain Lake Park on Tuesday afternoon. The still was located one block below the new auditorium on H street in a house owned by Mrs. Isabel Hill, of Washington, D. C., and which has been occupied for the past three months or more by Peter Davis, a Grecian, aged 38 years. The still was located in a front bed room on the upper floor while the mash and manufactured product was scattered about through various other portions of the building. The still was operated by gas. Upon the appearance of the officers, Davis, who was in the rear of the house shooting at a target, immediately abandoned the sport and beat it for the building. He entered a step ahead of the officers, shut and locked the door and took refuge in the attic. The officers, after they had gained access, spent some time in locating their quarry, but they were eventually successful and after a parley Davis appeared and surrendered. Immediately following his arrest on the dual charge of manufacturing and having intoxicating liquor in his possession for the purpose of sale, he was brought to Oakland and given a preliminary hearing before Justice W.A. Gonder, who fixed his bond at $700 for his appearance at the June Term of the Circuit Court. In default of bail, Davis was remanded to jail.

The officers, before bringing their prisoner to Oakland, destroyed the still, mash and the manufactured product.

The house was rented from Mrs. Hill by a man giving his name as George Stevens, of Fairmont, West Va., and according to residents of the Park, the lessee said he wanted it as a home for his wife, who was said to have suffered a 'nervous breakdown' and required the mountain air to restore her health.

There was nothing, according to the Park people, that would indicate that a still was in operation on the premises at any time prior to the arrival and raid made by the officers on Tuesday.

The still was one of fifty-gallon capacity and indications, according to the officers, was that it had been in use about three months.

Mrs. Isabel Hill owned the Maryland Home for many years; in the 1940s, she had the boarding house addition demolished and built two garages from the recovered material. She paid workman to build the first one, watching them closely. She built a duplicate garage herself; evidently, she was a quick study.[27] At some point she earned the nickname "the everlasting Mrs. Hill". This was either due to longevity, or her tendency to be a bit long-winded, or both.

In the 50s the house became two apartments, then around 1960, it returned to a single-family home, as it remains today.

The Elberon

The Elberon was built by Mr. William Henry Harrison Sheets, of Pittsburgh, Pa., in 1900 or 1901. There is one reference in the Republican paper of Mr. Sheets' house, "Wolton Cottage", being plastered in October 1901. Mr. Sheets was a businessman, founder of the Best, Fox, & Co., a manufacturer, in Pittsburgh. In 1907, Mr. Stone, of Wheeling, rented the Sheetz cottage.[28] Mr Stone's extended family owned several cottages in the Park.

In 1907 the Sheets Cottage was rented to Mr. William Scott of New York, hence the name on the photo below.[29] The first reference found of the cottage being named "The Elberon" is 1911.[30] Mr. Sheets passed away in 1912.

The Elberon ca. 1907. Courtesy of Bill and Tammy Ewing.

Around 1920, the sisters Misses Emma and Anna Hamill purchased the Elberon and operated the boarding house. Both sisters were school teachers, teaching at the Mt. Lake Park school and other local schools. Emma Hamill also served as Principal at a number of schools. The Hamill sisters owned and operated the Elberon until the late 1930s. The home was later converted to a private residence, owned by John Evans, Tammy Ewing's Grandfather.

The cottage still stands and is located at the corner of F and Oak Streets.

12 - THE "COTTAGES"

Many people ask, upon their first visit to the Park, "why are all these big houses called "Cottages"? If we look back to medieval times, the term cottage was used to refer to the small homes of "cotters" who lived on a manor, and had some land rights from the lord of the manor. By the late 1800's, the term was used, as in the case of Mt. Lake Park, to refer to vacation homes, to suggest a level of refinement and to distinguish the vacation homes from cabins.[1] And so, we have cottages that are quite large and a few that are humbler.

As mentioned, the early history of the park included an almost unimageable amount of building; the number of structures built in the 1880s and 1890s ranged from 20 to more than 30 houses, hotels and stores per year. We do not have space in this book to cover all the early cottages; we shall merely highlight some of them and save a more detailed look for another book.

MORE CLARKSBURGERS AT SUMMER RESORT

Where They Open Up Summer Cottages and Are Guests at the Hotels.

MT. LAKE PARK, Md., July 6— Misses Loeta and Mary Raymond, of Boston, daughters of Judge Raymond, of the supreme court, are visiting Mrs. John Ruhl, of Clarksburg, at her summer cottage here.
Mrs. J. W. Thorn, Mr. and Mrs. Harry Fernald and Mr. Jack Lewis, of Clarksburg, have opened up their summer cottage for the season.
H. E. Thalemen, of Clarksburg, made a short stop at the Loch Lynn Heights hotel.
Mrs. Henry Rapp and son, of Clarksburg, are visiting Mrs. Edward Davis at the Altamont cottage.
Charles E. Brooks and family, of Clarksburg, spent the last few days at the Loch Lynn hotel.

Clarksburg Telegram 7-6-1908

Carr Cottage

The Carr Cottage is certainly one of the first cottages in the Park; it was built in the summer of 1882, by Dr. Larned "Larney" Pitcher Carr, and his first wife Alice Hough from Fairmont, W. Va.[2] Mr. Carr was a druggist and in his early years he was a partner in the Logan-List Co. in Wheeling WV. The List family name has many connections to Mt. Lake; including A.S. List, one of the founders, and the hotel operator, Mr. List's daughter-in-law Mrs. L.B.C. List.

Carr Cottage ca. 1890, Courtesy of Sarah Haynes

"There was a young girl, Nell, that used to walk around the park quite often. She would regularly pick sweet peas at the fence in back of the Carr Cottage and then go around the front and sell them to Mrs. Carr." **Recalled by Mary Love**.

128

The "Cottages"

It is said that Larney built the Carr cottage for his mother, Mrs. L.E. Carr, of Fairmont. Larney Carr's brother, Dr. Logan Carr owned another cottage nearby, on G street, known as the **Cecil** cottage. Although they were only a block apart, the Carr brothers' had the first telephones installed in the Park., so as to reduce the "back and forth".

For more than 140 years, the Carr Cottage has only belonged to three families. The interior is much as it was in the late 1800's, with many of the original fixtures, and even the furniture intact. The current owners were kind enough to allow us to photograph the cottage interior and many of the objects inside. These photos can provide a glimpse of how summer residents lived in the late 19th century.

All photos on this and the following page courtesy of Sarah Haynes and Diana Runyan.

On the Porch of the Carr Cottage, Dr. Larney Carr seated in center. ca. 1895

Brunswick 'Victrola' ca. 1900. Might there have been *dancing* in the Carr Cottage?

This chair is visible in the photo on the previous page.

View of the Cecil/Lynndale (Logan Carr) Cottage ca. 1905 One of the earliest views of an auto in the Park. Courtesy of Sarah Haynes.

The "Cottages"

Original Ice Box, Carr Cottage

Eastlake style furniture set. This set was originally in the home now named the "Social Hall". (Formally Prevost Cottage)

A remarkable example of a 'deluxe' wash basin, ca. 1890. The entire top folds down, the "pitcher" tucks in. Below, one would place a bucket.

Magic Chef Gas Stove, still working.

Sad Iron for ironing, and hopefully not getting burned.

Original Ceiling Lamp ca. 1882

Formerly the Front Desk at the Mt. Lake Hotel, now a Kitchen Counter in the Carr Cottage.

Mr. and Mrs. "Larney" Carr ca. 1905. Likely Inez Maude Wills, Dr. Carr's second wife.

Old Liquor Bottles. Might there have been *drinking* in the Carr Cottage?

Sarah Haynes tells us, *"When my family purchased the house around 1960, there were hundreds of liquor bottles tucked away in the corners of the attic."* Presumably, the former occupants were afraid to dispose of these elsewhere, for fear of losing their house.

The "Cottages"

Hayden Cottage

The Hayden Cottage was built in 1885 by Mr. Lorenzo T. Yoder, from Pittsburgh, Pa. Mr. Yoder was a businessman, specifically in the candy business in Pennsylvania. In 1883, Mr. Yoder patented a candy crimper which made it much easier (the advert says a young boy could use it) to make ribbon candy.[3] With this candy business, Mr. Yoder became a very wealthy man. He built a 400-room hotel in Pittsburgh, *"The Yoder Hotel, for men only, no Liquor on Premises."* L.T. was a devout person and a staunch supporter of Prohibition. Naturally, he liked what he saw in Mt. Lake Park. He was one of the early association stock holders; after Mr. Yoder built what is now named the Hayden Cottage, he went on to create the "water works", and in 1900, he bought the Mt. Lake Hotel.

Hayden Cottage ca. 1980

L to R Elizabeth, Hillis, Elcy

Advert for Candy Machine

L.T. Yoder when a young man. Photos retrieved from Yodernewsletter.org

Three of Mr. Yoder's children at the "Tiffany Lady", another house he built. Early Park residents paid their water bills at this house.

The Hayden Cottage was rented out in the early to mid-1890s. Several families rented it, including the Ruhl family, just before their cottage was built across the street.

In later years, around 1904, Mr. Yoder was at odds with the other Association stockholders. He wanted the Association to recognize the changing times and loosen up some of the 'hidebound" regulations. The Association refused his request; this will be covered in more detail later in this book.

Now, to turn our attention to Mr. Hayden of Hayden cottage;[4] Captain James Hayden was a Union officer in the Civil War, captured during that conflict, and the founder of The Republican newspaper. He published the paper from 1877 until 1890, when he sold it to Benjamin H. Sincell.[5] Capt. Hayden then retired from the newspaper business and moved to Mt. Lake. The Hayden family initially lived in the cottage named Haydenhurst, across the street from what is now called Hayden Cottage. He and his wife, Lititia, later purchased the Hayden Cottage from L.T. Yoder around the turn of the century.

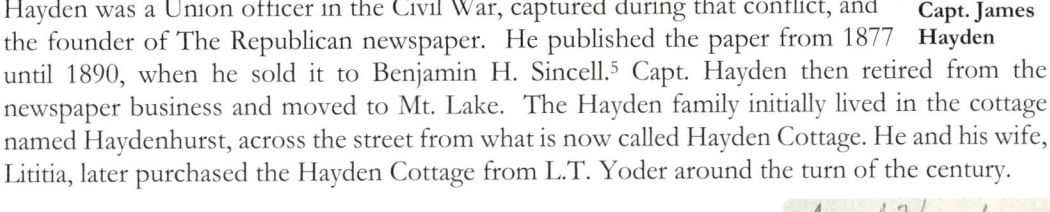

Capt. James Hayden

On March 3, 1877 in the first issue of the paper, Mr. Haden wrote:
"With today's issue we commence the publication of The Republican which we are warranted in saying (we hope it shall) hereafter be a permanent institution in our community and which propose to make a welcome week visitor to every household in the County." Mr. Hayden certainly achieved his goal.

131

The "Cottages"

Around 1901, Mr. Hayden's sons, J.Grant and Lee Hayden, operated a grocery store near the Columbian Hotel.[6] J. Grant would go on to start a grocery store in Westernport, Md.

After 1900, Mr. Hayden was an appointed Special Agent of the U.S. Dept. of Agriculture; he traveled extensively throughout Maryland, inspecting crops. He also served as a member of the Maryland House of Delegates for a number of years.[7] Capt. Hayden died in 1931.

Stone Cottage(s)

The Stone family and their six generations of descendants owned several cottages in the Park, we will cover some of them here. The Cottage on the corner of G and Oak Streets, known as the **Stone Cottage**, was built in 1884 by Elijah J. Stone. Mr. Stone was a merchant from Wheeling W.Va. He and his brother-in-law, J.C. Thomas, started a dry goods store. This business would become Stone and Thomas, a large department store chain in W. Va.

Mr. Stone was a devout Methodist, Minister of the Thompson M.E. Church on Wheeling Island and as such was attracted to Mt. Lake; as soon as their first summer cottage was built, the family began spending their summers here.[8] It is said that the windows of the Stone Cottage, which don't quite match, were salvaged from a great flood on Wheeling Island and shipped to Mt. Lake.

Stone Cottage ca. 1979 Photo Courtesy of Mary Love

E.J. Stone also built the Cottage next door to the Stone Cottage, now known as the **J.Sumner Stone Cottage**.

J.Sumner Stone Cottage ca. 1906 J.Sumner Standing, wife Kate Elson Stone in chair next to steps. Daughter Marybai Stone sitting on top steps, right side. Photo courtesy of Beverly Robinson. In later years, Mary Love lived in this cottage.

The "Cottages"

E.J Stone died in 1887 at the age of 67; E.J.'s wife, Elizabeth, inherited the property. In 1892, when Elizabeth died, J.Sumner Stone, formally inherited his cottage.[9] J.Summner and his wife, Kate, would own this cottage for the next 32 years. Although he was trained as a medical doctor, J.Sumner Stone could not resist the call to do missionary work. He and his wife, Kate, traveled the world, J.Sumner was the President for International Missionary Union, and Kate was the Secretary and Treasurer of the Woman's Foreign Missionary Society for nearly 25 years. In their travels, they encountered many hardships and adventures.

They did make time to visit the Park in the summertime; Beverly Railey Robinson describes one popular event, produced by Kate:[10]

Kate, who had exceptional "people skills", valued the customs of the people with whom she worked. As she traveled throughout the world, she collected costumes of native people from all the countries she visited.

One summer, at Mt. Lake, Kate developed a special pageant called the "Trip Around the World in Sixty Minutes". Young men and women were dressed in costumes she provided, and the program was such a success that it was repeated at Wheeling and many other cities.

In 1910, a daughter-in-law of E.J. and Elizabeth, wife of Llewellyn Stone and also named Elizabeth, bought the S.L. Allen property, one of the first Cottages in the Park.[11] This cottage is situated diagonally from the original Stone Cottage. This property became known as the Gables. The Gables has been in the Stone family ever since, 113 years and counting.

Mr. E.J. Stone did not stop after building a couple of cottages; he also built more than five rental cottages in the area that would become known as "Cozy Row." (Initially spelled "Cosey Row"). These cottages were initially numbered "Stone Cottage No. 1, 2, 3", etc., and were built around 1885, Mr. Stone improved them in 1886 and 1887.

> The Arnold Bro.'s have contracted with Mr. E. J. Stone to plaster his remaining five cottages in Cosey Row. This will make them tenable in winter as well as summer.

From the Republican, May 12, 1887. Initially these cottages and many other buildings were not "plastered"; there was just the exterior wall to keep out the elements.

An early view of "Cozy Row" on E street. The cottage on the left became known as "Journey's End." In the early years there was a bakery in at least one of these cottages.

COZY ROW ON E. STREET

The two Stone Cottages are still with us, as are some of the "Cosey Row" cottages. The descendants of E.J. Stone later became very active in the Mt. Lake Tennis Tournaments; they host social events associated with the tournament to this day.

Byrne-Sincell Cottage

The following information is provided with permission of the Sincell family. This picture and Facebook posting is from Mary Sincell McEwen in October, 2022.

Mary Sincell McEwen
20h

I love this photo. It is of a house on H Street in Mountain Lake Park that still stands and is in use. Mrs. Mary Anne Byrne had it built in the late 1880s. She is pictured in the rocking chair. She was my great-great-great grandmother. From left are Julia Byrne, sister to Mary Anne; Lillian "Tay" Morris Sincell; and her mother Eleanor Byrne. This was taken probably in about 1890. The family was from Kingwood but spent many summers at the MLP Chautauqua. Tay married Benjamin Hinkle Sincell, owner and editor of The Republican newspaper from 1890 until his death in 1947. She was very civically active with St. Mark's Lutheran Church, the Civic Club of Oakland, and the suffrage movement. **See less**

Mary Sincell McEwen was the Senior Writer at The Republican newspaper for many years. We have leaned on the Republican newspaper for so many stories and for fact-checking, we thought we would just include this posting in its entirety. Mary Sincell McEwen passed away on November 17, 2022, a few weeks after this post.

Altamont Cottage

The Altamont Cottage was located on M street, diagonal to the still-standing Lee Cottage. The Hardys were early visitors to Mt. Lake. Mr. C.S. Hardy died in 1888, in the Park. Sometime after Mr. Hardy's death, this house was built by Mrs. Kate (Vincent). Hardy. Mrs. Hardy had some family connection to the Weber family, but we are not sure of the exact relationship. Mrs. Hardy rented out the cottage for more than thirty years, starting in 1893. Around 1900, Mrs. Hardy rented this cottage to Virginia Governor and former Confederate General Fitzhugh Lee and family.[12]

> A dispatch from Cumberland, Md., says: "General Fitzhugh Lee has leased the Altamont Cottage at Mountain Lake Park for this season, and this week moved there with his family." General Lee is still in Cuba.

Tazewell, Va. Republican 7-19-1900

Shortly after the summer of 1901, Mrs. Hardy rented the cottage to Mr. Edwin Reazin Davis, Sr. The Davis' of Clarksburg, were relatives of the Maxwell's and the Jarvis family. Mr. Davis' family then rented the cottage for the following _21_ summers.[13] Mr. Davis entertained many prominent people at the cottage, including the former Governor of W.Va., George W. Atkinson's family.

Altamont Cottage ca. 1906. Courtesy of Bill Davis and J.Horner Davis IV.

These face-to-face swings, sometimes called "expression gliders", are seen in many of the old photos of Mt. Lake Park, but usually at a distance. Here, in 1907, we have a closeup view of the swing at Altamont Cottage. Note the croquet mallet and other yard toys strewn about.

E.R.Davis children, possibly E.R. Davis, Jr. and JHorner Davis II ca. 1907. Courtesy J.Horner Davis IV.

On the Porch, Altamont Cottage, ca. 1907. Woman in white, right-center, with black bow, Garnett Horner Davis. Two boys in right-front, thought to be E.R. Davis, Jr. and J.Horner Davis II. J.Horner Davis II would become a prominent attorney, serving as Delegate and Majority Leader of the W. Va. House of Representatives. In the 1940s-1950s, he would also become co-owner of both the Maxwell and Seldon Cottages in the Park.

Mrs. Hardy continued to visit the park and rent out her cottage, well after the Davis family stopped renting it. Mrs. Kate V. Hardy (Hardie) died on Dec. 26, 1937. Her cottage was ultimately torn down. She is buried in the Oakland Cemetery.

Ruhl Cottage

The Ruhl Cottage is a Queen Anne Victorian structure built in 1895 by the Bradford Brothers Planing Mill of Oakland, for Mrs. Mary F. Walker. The cost to build the home ran just a bit over $1600.00 It was a gift to her daughter Julia, who married John Ruhl of Clarksburg, W. Va. The Ruhl family would own the cottage for the next 82 years.[14]

Julia Walker Ruhl was a leader in the Women's Suffrage movement and President of the West Virginia Equal Rights Suffrage Association. Julia was also the founder of the Clarksburg, W.Va. library. She was active in the Park, a leader in the Park Civic Club, the Tennis Club, and founder of the Mt. Lake library.

Portrait hanging in Waldomere, the Clarksburg Library, founded by Julia Walker Ruhl.

Ruhl Cottage ca. 1900. Courtesy of Karen Wooddell.

Historical Marker at the Ruhl Cottage.

Julia Ruhl's children in the carriage, Henry, Mary (center), and Rebecca (right) near the Tabernacle, ca. 1905. Courtesy of Karen Wooddell.

The Ruhl Cottage still stands; it has been owned by the same family for the last 56 years.

The "Cottages"

Maxwell Cottage

The Maxwell Cottage was built in 1901 by Mr. and Mrs. William Brent Maxwell of Clarksburg, W. Va. The Maxwell's were a wealthy family, with large land and mining interests. Mr. Maxwell was also the founder of the Union National Bank of Clarksburg and the Union Bank of Union, W.Va. Mr. Maxwell's 2nd wife, Lillian Jarvis Maxwell, was a (distant) cousin of Anna Jarvis, credited with inventing "Mother's Day".

Lillian B. Jarvis Maxwell, ca 1916

W.B. Maxwell, ca. 1877

Maxwell Cottage ca. 1902. Maxwell Children on the porch, unknown servant standing.

Back caption reads, "Ruth, Frank and Bill (Maxwell) and Ella Jackson, their nurse for many years."

Eastlake set, thought to be original to the Maxwell Cottage.

A gathering at Maxwell Cottage, ca. 1920. They are likely watching tennis; from their vantage one could watch the action on the Maxwell court as well as the Tennis Tournament across the street. Some possible people are Bill Steadman, far left, Julia Ruhl, center, looking left, and thought to be Henry Ruhl, right.

The Maxwell's daughter, Ruth Maxwell, went on to marry Louis P. Johnson, the Secretary of Defense in the Truman administration.

The Maxwell's owned their Cottage for 75 years. It still stands today.

Creedmore

Creedmore was built in 1903-1904 by another West Virginian, Mr. Creed Brice Collins, hailing from Pennsboro W. Va. Mr. Collins was a Confederate veteran of the Civil War; he later became a successful merchant in Ritchie County, W. Va., and at one time, was regarded as the wealthiest man in that section. Mr. Collins owned "Collins Company" and was a founder and President of the First National Bank of Pennsboro. He built a large home in Pennsboro, named "Oak Hall", and had extensive land holdings there.

After the turn of the century, and just after building Creedmore, Mr. Collins incurred financial losses, said to be no fault of his own, and eventually lost nearly everything. As a result of this strain, his health broke down; he died in 1909.[15]

Creedmore, 1906, from Birds-eye map, Courtesy of Library of Congress

His wife, Mrs. Susan (Haymond) Collins, continued to visit the Park and owned the Cottage until 1919. Mrs. Collins rented the Cottage out after her husband died; in 1916, we find a "Help Wanted"advert, "Girl for General Housework, no washing, Wages $5.50 per week.[16] The ad was placed by a Mrs. Susan Hartman. In the winter of 1916, Mr. and Mrs. Ralph Weber rented the cottage.[17]

The Creedmore still stands; it has had several owners over the decades, the present owners have occupied the house for more than 46 years.

Creedmore on left, looking west on Oakland Dr. Note the face-to-face swing in the background. These swings are described earlier.

Creed Collins and Family, ca 1892. Creed Collins on left, wife Susan Haymond Collins sitting next to Creed.

Photo above retrieved from
http://www.geo-met.com/tommysmith/creed.htm

13 - *THE* MOUNTAIN LAKE

The founders were committed to building a lake from the outset of planning the summer resort. In the winter of 1881-1882, they constructed a temporary dam on Broadford Run, to create some ponding, which would freeze. The objective was to create and harvest enough ice for the first summer of 1882.

> —The Mountain Lake Park Association have made a temporary dam across Broadford run, on their grounds, with the expectation of securing ice for use next season. They are constructing an ice house with a capacity of about 400 tons.
>
> The Republican Jan. 7, 1882.
> The 1st attempt at damming Broadford run, for Ice.

The actual creation of the lake had been something of a mystery, but we now have these facts: In the fall of 1882, the Association awarded a contract to "Mr. J.L. Burley, of Moundsville" to dig a lake and dam the Broadford Run Stream. By Oct. 21, 1882, Mr. Burley was fully engaged in this effort and was looking for more manpower to help him dig.

> Mr. Burley, of Moundsville, began work on the lake yesterday. He expects to complete the work in about four weeks. He still wants more help from those who are not ashamed to dig.

The Republican Oct. 21, 1882

The Mountain Lake, after 1900. The Ice House and Electric Plant appear in the background. Road in the foreground leads up to the Crystal Spring.

The Mountain Lake

Mr. Burley fulfilled his contract for creating the lake in the Fall and Winter of 1882. Initially, the lake was very small, only 9 or 10 acres in size, not much more than a large pond. (In subsequent years it would be enlarged, as shown in the photo below)

Birds-eye view of the Mountain Lake, after being enlarged. ca. 1920

Mr. Burley also made arrangements with the Association to set up the first ice harvesting operation at the lake. By the winter of 1882, he had built a small ice house on the western side of the lake. (On the left side of the Lake in the photo, above.) This initial ice harvesting operation was likely for local use, as the building was small and the distance to the B & O railroad line would impede attempts to ship large quantities via rail. In later years, the ice operation would scale up, with a much larger ice house on the eastern side of the lake and its own rail side track, allowing increased production.

In the 1880s, the lake was a rather quiet spot, with limited recreational activities, but the Association made big plans in 1893, to expand the lake and offer boating, bathing and other amenities.[1] After 1894, when the lake improvements were completed, the lake was approximately 50 acres in size. A narrow road encircled the lake. On brief tour around the lake (ideally via carriage) one would find a bathhouse near the dam, further north was a manmade island with boat house.

The island and boat house were connected to the shore by a wooden bridge. (See bridge photo in this chapter.) As you moved up the lake via "Lake Shore drive", there was the Crystal Spring, a popular picnic spot. (More on the crystal spring later.) From Crystal spring the road would cross Broadford run, then turn south, along the eastern side of the lake. On the eastern side was a caretaker's house, the ice house, and below the dam a power plant and baseball fields. A road was built across the dam and spillway and this was one of the primary roads to Deer Park and beyond.

> Work on the enlargement of the lake will begin in earnest in a few days. As soon as the ice house can be emptied it will be taken down and put up on the east side of the lake. The lake will be made so as to gather a crop of ice this winter.

**The Republican Sept. 20, 1894
Lake Enlargement Project Commences.**

In the late 1890s, there was a strong emphasis on sporting and leisure activities at the lake. You could rent a boat, life buoy (presumably for those not comfortable with swimming.), motor boat (in later years), or a swimsuit. (See boat house photo for prices.) You could do all this and more, but not on Sunday. As the sign on a later page says, "boating and bathing forbidden on Sunday".

The Mountain Lake

Boaters and Bathers, Mt. Lake, Ca 1910. Looking South towards the Dam, Ice House ramp and Electric Power Plant in upper left-hand corner.

The lake and boats underwent a significant upgrade again in 1911. The following update is provided in the June 1st 1911 edition of The Republican:

> *The lake, it is hoped, will be more attractive this year. The launch and row boats are being completely renovated and put in first class condition: the landings rebuilt, and the launch house restored to perpendicular. But the main change is the developing of the island into what it is hoped will be quite a resort feature. A rustic foot bridge extends from the mainland to the westside of the island, and a Bungalow Bath House has been erected on the south east "corner." A floor in the shallow part of the lake with appropriate stairs and platform of approach, giving ample opportunities for the uninitiated to be inducted into the swimming art, while two spring boards over the main channel provides for the daring and diving experts. A pergola on the highest part of the island will give shelter to those who on our hot days want to enjoy the cool breezes that blow here as no where else in the "Park."*
>
> *The H. Weber & Sons Co. have consented to take on the landscape gardening. The beds have been laid out by Mr. Will McRobie, and under his supervision the Weber's will make the island a bower of beauty before the summer crowds appear.*

Note the addition of a "platform" to make it easier for swimmers. In later years, residents such as Betty Randol described this wooden platform as a welcome improvement so one could avoid the muddy lake bottom.

Bridge to the island and boat house, ca. 1905.

Boating and Bathing Forbidden on Sunday -For Hire/Per Hour-Boats, Lifebouy,Swimsuits

Swimming and Boating ca. 1914

Swimming at Mt. Lake ca. 1914

Goldsbourgh Collection, Courtesy Garrett Historical Society

Two of the challenges of swimming at Mt. Lake were the muddy bottom of the lake and the general murkiness of the water. In the photo on the left, the ladies appear to be showing off their footwear, an early version of water shoes. Mary Love recalled, *"You learned to swim pretty quick if you stepped off into the muddy bottom!"*

Early Postcard of the Bridge over the Lake Spillway, with Wood and Iron Bridge ca 1910.

School children on outing. Newer spillway bridge formed with concrete – ca.1950 Sarah Steyer's Grandmother, Mable Porter Sollars was a school teacher at the Mt. Lake School around 1950., this is thought to be her class. Courtesy of Sarah Steyer.

Spillway remnants in winter, 2022. The stonework and roadbed remain.

Different view of the lake, looking South. Power Plant, Rail line and Ice House on left. Boat house, Island, and Foot Bridge in center - After 1900.

The Mountain Lake

The 1906 Birds-eye view map below shows the athletic fields, primarily used for baseball, and the Power Plant below the dam. To the left of the dam, besides a boat house and swimming platform, was an Association cottage and, further left, a campground. On the right side of the lake, above the dam, is the Ice House and side track.

Closer view of the lake from the 1906 map. Courtesy of Library of Congress.

Ice House ca. 1918 Courtesy of the B & O Museum, Baltimore, Md.

The photo above was retrieved from the B & O Museum in Baltimore. It provides one of the best views of the Ice House as seen from the dam. This photo is noteworthy for the electric pole and wires from the Power Plant and the fact that it is a summertime view.

The Mountain Lake

Quiet at Mt. Lake - Photo may have been taken on a Sunday.

Caretaker House Mountain Lake, built in 1895

    This house was situated on Mt. Lake and early descriptions name it the "Caretaker's House", for a man who will have "charge of the Lake".[2] The exact location of the house is unknown, although it was thought to be on the eastern side of the lake. In the Martha Grimes novels, set in Mt. Lake, a house on the eastern side of the lake figures prominently. In her novels it was abandoned, much like the lake itself today, and always shrouded in mystery.

1940s, Cousins Mimi (Davis) Degrafft & Margo (Davis) Scott babysitting their teacher's children. Courtesy of Mimi Degrafft.

2002 The marshy (former) lakebed. Photo by Martha Kahl.

The lake was created by an earthen dam; the dam was generally unstable and had to be repaired after the many rainstorms and floods over the years. After the 1940s, periodic repairing of the dam ceased and the lake would only occasionally be filled with excess rainfall. Finally, in the 1980s, the dam was permanently breached and once again the lake became a marshy "glade".

Boathouse Rental Prices, Suits 25 cents/hr.

14 - THE CRYSTAL SPRING

It is presumed that the crystal spring near the Mountain Lake has flowed for hundreds, if not thousands of years. Early association minutes describe plans to "develop" the crystal spring for the enjoyment of summer visitors. In the summer of 1883, a "ramble and drive" were being added along the lake to allow carriage rides to the springs. This drive was completed and graded in April of 1884.[1] The spring development went through many incarnations over the decades; it was a popular destination from the 1880s on through the 1970s. Located on the western slope of Broadford run, it was one of the feeders of the Mountain Lake and also an early source of water for the resort.

Around 1885, the association dug out a quiet pool just below the spring. Although overgrown, the pool still exists and the spring still flows.

Some stories are told of how there was always a tin cup in a stone inset just above the spring. Perhaps the thirsty visitor in the above photo is using the tin cup. For decades, many locals coveted the spring water and would only drink water from the crystal spring.

Footpath to Crystal Springs - Postcard

Side view of the Crystal Spring.

A Photo of Crystal Spring ca. 1918. Courtesy of the B & O Museum, Baltimore.
The building towards the left is not seen in any other photos of the spring. Around 1900, Mr. L.T. Yoder built a pump house and used the water from the spring for his Mt. Lake "water works". This may be the "pump house".

Children's outing to Crystal Spring at Mountain Lake, ca. 1950 Courtesy of Sarah Steyer.

Crystal Spring in the 1950's.

Above, the Spring during an early period of neglect.

Right, the Crystal Spring in 2022, abandoned, but still flowing.

15 - WINTERTIME

The Colonial Boarding House in Winter[1]

In the early years, Mountain Lake Park in winter was a deserted place. After all, it was a summer resort. When the Park was first conceived, the founders didn't really imagine many people "wintering over". In the first decade there were just a handful of families and "care takers" staying on. To illustrate this point: Mt. Lake Park's electric power plant was first built out around 1900. For nearly 20 years after 1900, the electric company, Garrett Water and Light, shut the electric off after the summer season.[2] There were practical reasons for this; they simply didn't have enough electric consumers to justify firing the plant boilers all winter long.

Old Park Library Sign once hung in The Colonial Boarding House
Courtesy Bill and Tammy Ewing

Wintertime

When winter set in, many of the public buildings did not have heat, such as the bowling alley/summer library, located near the tennis courts (What is now town hall.). Each fall season, the library books would be carried to one of the year-round houses, ofttimes the Colonial, sometimes the Hayden cottage, and the library would be relocated. The winter residents could make an appointment with "Miss Josie" Weimer to check out their books. In the spring, the books would be transported back to the bowling alley for a new summer season.

"KING ICE"

"They drained the lake in the fall and let it fill with clear water for ice. The B and O took out car after carload." **Ed Lewis remembers**.

Ice was the cash crop of winter in the Park. By opening a valve at the spillway, the water from the lake would be drained in late fall, and the lake would then be refilled. This helped reduce the algae and organic material that built up during the summer months and made the "crystal clear" ice possible. (If the reader wants to get a sense of the nature of the Mt. Lake water, take a look at the water in current Broadford Lake during late Summer-murky!) Ice harvesting was a good source of income for farm workers and others during the winter months but it could be brutal. The harvesting season generally started in late November or early December and, for volume production, the temperature needed to be around 0 degrees Fahrenheit to produce ice blocks 9-12 inches thick.

Ice Harvesting tools, retrieved from historicsoduspoint.com/commerce/ice-harvesting

ICE,
Mountain Lake Park, Md.
CUT FROM CRYSTAL SPRING WATER,
WHOLESALE ONLY.
Address
Mountain Lake Park Association,
MOUNTAIN LAKE PARK, MD.

Large Ice House at Mt. Lake Ca. 1900

When the lake and dam were first constructed, Mr. J.L. Burley had a small ice house and ice harvesting operation on the west side of the lake. The ice would be cut with saws by hand, then the "ice cakes" would be stored in layers in the ice house, with each layer separated by sawdust. Mr. Burley's ice operation was fairly small and the ice was used by the local hotels and summer visitors.

Harvesting ice at Mt. Lake

From Once upon a Mountiantop. This picture appears to be "posed" as the gentlemen in the center is wearing a suit and tie (and no gloves). The other men appear to be the actual workers.

"As I remember it, there was an old ice house, over on that (far) side of the lake, they cut these big, deep blocks of ice. They used horses that would go out on the lake, and some how or other they cut those blocks of ice. The horse would pull a sled with a knife." **Betty Randol remembers.**

The availability of ice was a key ingredient for the success of the summer resort. Even a rumor of a shortage of ice could reduce the number of summer visitors to the park.[3]

Prior to mechanized refrigeration, the B & O railroad always had a strong demand for ice, and they had an agreement with the Association granting the railroad rights to 50% of the ice harvesting in Mt. Lake. After 1894, when the lake was enlarged, the B &O built a sideling track to the Eastern side of the lake where a larger ice house was constructed. This larger ice house and rail cars be seen in pictures in this chapter. With the need for larger volumes of ice, a more efficient means of ice harvesting was required. Thus enters the "ice sled" that Betty Randol remembered. In 1898 Superintendent Rudisell purchased an ice plow and other labor-saving tools.[4] The ice plow was hitched to a horse and the lake ice was scored or "plowed" in a grid pattern. After the grooves in the ice were cut deep enough, the ice harvesters could take saws and pikes and break off the ice blocks and float them towards the ice house.

A description found in The Cumberland Times provides details on the Mountain Lake ice harvesting process. The ice was loaded into rail cars and shipped to Cumberland and Brunswick, Maryland and stored for future use.

"The association has the railroad contract and the scope of it seems unlimited. One winter not long ago 3000 (rail) carloads were shipped as fast as it was cut and the storage house on the lake bank, holding 2000 carloads was filled to be used later as needed."

"The ice makes steady work for large number of men and boys during the ordinary winters. As fast as the lake is cut over it freezes again and the job is the same thing over again from early winter until almost spring. The wages average $4.00 per day and the work comes in handy for those who live permanently in the resort. (The lake) freezes hard and permanently and is noted for how hard it lasts. The railroad company puts the provision into the contract that no cakes shall be less than 9 inches thick when loaded into the cars. This is hardly necessary however, for the average cut is usually double the thickness."

"Cutting the ice from the surface of the lake has been gotten down to a system. The first thing down is to run a horse drawn plow over the surface, marking off squares the size the cakes are to be cut. It is no uncommon sight to see one or more good sized horses on the lake."

"Cutters armed with saws follow, keeping to the lines made by the ploughs. Then push boys follow. With iron pointed poles they punch the cakes through channels to the hoisting outfit near where the cars are loaded and there the cakes are either placed in the waiting cars or in the huge storage house."

"It is a rule with those in charge of harvesting the ice to give employment to practically every man and boy who seeks the work. For this reason, several score are employed at one time. On big days the surface of the lake is literally covered with the dark forms of the harvesters." **From the Cumberland Times, February, 1925.**

Nov. 1908

Supt. Davis Wednesday gave the force working at the ice plant a turkey dinner. The dinner was prepared and served at the Long cottage near the lake.

Ice Plow example, retrieved from antiqueicetoolmuseum.org

Thursday morning last a force went to work on the lake cutting ice, but they had to give it up before night, after loading two cars and storing a few tons in the ice house. The horse which was being used in the ice plow broke through the ice and was gotten to the shore with some difficulty. If the present cold "snap" should produce ice six inches thick or more the plant will be run to its utmost capacity both day and night.

Horse falls through Ice - Clip from the Mt. Lake column, the Republican Feb. 11, 1909.

This approach to ice harvesting could be found in communities throughout the North, but it was full of hazards. Below is an article clipped from the Republican paper in 1909.

AN ITALIAN KILLED SUNDAY.

Was Engaged in Cutting Ice at Mountain Lake Park.

Sunday morning an Italian, employed by the Baltimore and Ohio in cutting and loading ice at Mountain Lake Park, fell under a moving car and was decapitated. The man had jumped on the car and was clinging to the hand rail as the train was being pushed into position along the lake shore when he was struck by a pile of snow alongside the track which broke his hold. He was thrown to the track, a car passing over him and killing him instantly. A fellow laborer, also an Italian, had a narrow escape with his life, he too being thrown from the car but escaping with no injuries of moment.

The dead man's remains were brought to Oakland and interred in the Catholic cemetery.

The Republican Feb. 20, 1902

It is notable that the man killed in this article is identified as an "Italian". In the early 1900s, Italian immigrants faced heavy discrimination and had no choice but to take the jobs that others would not. The same can be said of the racial discrimination that African Americans faced; it is said that blacks were employed in the ice harvesting operations at Mt. Lake Park as well.

Betty Randol tells of another time when her father, Hebert Leighton, was involved in supervising the ice harvesting and fell through the ice:

> *Well, he was out there, 'telling them how to do it' and he slid off through the ice. I can't imagine how he got home without his clothes all being frozen to him. We were all so worried about him, catching pneumonia and whatnot, but somehow, he came though it alright."*

An advertisement for an early refrigerator railcar.
(Image: Mid-Continent Railway Museum)

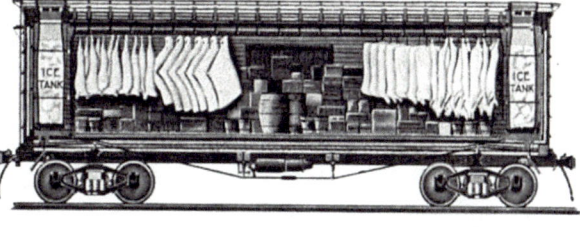

A cut-away view of an early version of a refrigerator railcar, circa 1870s.
(Image: National Railroad Museum)

The illustrations above show how important ice was in shipping perishables.[5]

The ice house(s) burned down a few times; each time the cause appeared to be unknown, but suspicious. Perhaps the most spectacular Ice House fire took place in June of 1908.[6] The Ice house was full of ice for the summer season and the fire damage was total. All that was left was a large pile of ice where the building once stood. The association was able to salvage the ice for the upcoming summer season.

Ice House, Mt. Lake Park, ca. 1905. Railcars visible in the background, under the conveyer.

As the summer resort transitioned to a year-round town, there were more people living in the park in winter. The need for ice decreased because of new refrigeration; the winter lake grew quieter and more leisurely activities such as ice skating and sled riding were common in winter.

"We used to go sled riding, down the hill by the Maxwell Cottage, sometimes we could coast all the way down to Pilgrims' Rest," recalled **Mary Love.**

Wintertime

As nearly as we can sort out, the house in this picture was owned by Mr. Fouch, the telegraph operator at the depot. There is a photo of Mr. Fouch in the chapter on the railroad.

"We would build a big bonfire on the shore and skate at the lake," remembered **Betty Randol**. *"Sometimes we would skate down by Pilgrims' Rest as well."*

Ice Skating at Mt. Lake, illustration by Karen Fichter.

16 - ELECTRIC, WATER & SEWERS, OH MY!

Before we review the first modern improvements in Mt. Lake Park infrastructure, it may be useful to mention the "state of the art" before 1900. Every house, boarding house, and hotel needed a well and pump, and one or more "Necessary Rooms". And at night, in a world lit only by fire, they needed plenty of lamps.

Well Pump, Outhouse & Lamp. Still present, but not in use…

Courtesy of Mary Jane Berry and Robert Ulino

Courtesy of Jim and Jenny Neville

Outdoor Lanterns at the Superintendent's House in front of Assembly Hall Ca. 1890

Chamber Pots, Courtesy of Sarah Haynes

Electric Pole Near the Lake ca. 1915

Electric

Electric lighting first came to the Park in 1894, when an electric line was strung from Oakland. This extension from Oakland was a limited effort and it was used to provide outside lighting to the "grove", around the Assembly Hall.[1] After an early effort to create the Park's own power plant, in 1901, another corporation, "Garrett Electric Power and Light" was formed.

This group, led by L.A. Rudisill and P.T. Garthwright along with the Attorney F.A. Thayer, brought successful power generation and electric distribution to the Park.[2]

When electric lighting and distribution came about, there was no hard rule that only one set of distribution wires could be installed in a place like Mt. Lake Park. In the early years, there were two different companies supplying electric to the Park, "Park Water & Light", and "Garrett Water and Light". These two companies co-existed for a number of years, with each of them running their own electric wires on poles throughout the park. (Much like the early days of the telephone, where there were several companies building out the same distribution lines.) The Park Water and Light company was first in the park, but it appears they ultimately lost out to Garrett Water and Light. This may have been because the Park Water and Light actually operated the first water system in the Park; it was plagued by problems and likely damaged the Park Water and Light company's reputation.

The Power Plant, looking south, located just below the Lake dam.

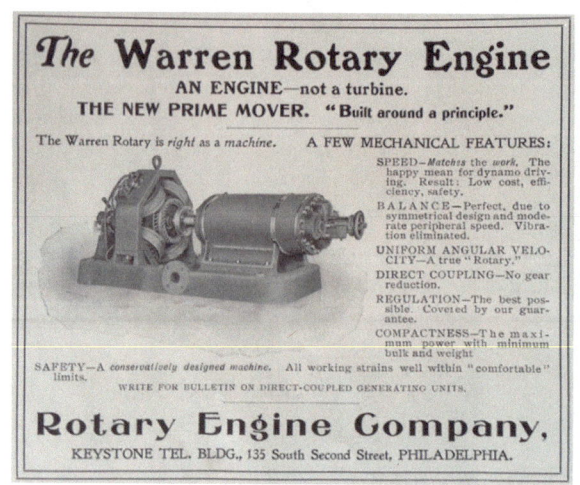

Example of early Knob & Tube wiring in Mt Lake. Early wiring consisted of a single 110 volt circuit for the whole house. Photo Courtesy of Steve Cowgill.

In 1902, a Warren Engine and Dynamo generated 110 volt Electric for the Park. From The Republican, June 19, 1902, a detailed write up of the new electric lighting:

160

NEW ELECTRIC LIGHTS
The Garrett Water and Light Company Plant at the Park.

Bulb from old Bowling Alley

Last Thursday the Garrett Water and Light Company had its plant completed and ready for operation and for the first time turned on the current and brilliantly lighted up the Park and numerous cottages. The plant is one of the best of its size as to machinery and construction in the State. It has the highest ideas involved in electric lighting, having a dynamo efficiency of 98 per cent. The machine has a voltage of 2200 transformed down to 110 volts. The wiring is in three series, so arranged that the line furnishing light to the hotels and houses, etc., can be placed in service independent of the street lines.

The lamps furnish a very bright, clear light and everybody has a word of praise for their brilliancy. The four-valve slow speed engine is a magnificent piece of machinery, almost noiseless in its movements and moves like the works of a watch.

Said one of the leading citizens of Oakland last evening: "I have visited a great many electric light plants but never saw as perfect a plant as this." | Said another gentleman speaking of the engine: "It is as fine as silk." The plant is well worth a visit by anyone interested in machinery.

The building is a two story house, the second being used for a store room. South of the boiler room and connected with the boiler room is a large coal house having a capacity of 70 tons of coal. The power house is located on the side track running from the B. & O. road to the ice house, thus enabling the Light Company to have its coal put right at the plant.

Among the houses using the service of the new company are the following: The Hicks House, 43 lights; Hustling Store Co., the drug store, Hotel Chautauqua, 45 lights; Braethorn, 17 lights; W. H. H. Sheets, Mrs. M. Haymond, Thomas Deveny, L. C. Carr, F. T. Martin, Mrs. Talson's two cottages, L. A. Rudisill, C. W. Hopkins, P. T. Garthright, etc.

The company has three men wiring houses and contracts ahead to keep the employees busy for some time to come. The Tabernacle in which the Y. M. C. A. Convention was held was beautifully lighted by 19 32-candle power lamps and 5 16-candle power lamps. The Park is lighted by 125 32-candle power lamps. The water supply for the boiler is secured from the lake. The water comes to the plant by gravity.

There is a feeling of relief because the erection of this plant guarantees an abundance of water for all purposes at the Park. Should the Mountain Lake Water Company fail to supply water this summer as it did last season it is the intention of the new company to lay pipe throughout the Park next fall and furnish water to the citizens of that community, having sufficient power not only to produce electricity, but to pump millions of gallons of water daily.

The Park Water and Light Company Advertisement, about 1900.
The Company was an early electric provider for the Park.

The Park Water and Light Company ultimately lost out to Garrett Water and Light as the dominate electric provider in Mt. Lake.

By 1911, the Park still enjoyed electric lighting <u>only during the Summer</u>. It must have been a serious undertaking to "fire up" the electric plant after it was off for eight months, especially as it was off all during the winter storms. This write up in the Republican provides a glimpse of the effort to get the electric going for the 1911 season:[3]

> The opening of the residence season, which takes place this week, June 1st, is a quiet affair, and attended with no other formality than the starting of the electric light plant and the running of the ice wagon. Electrician Hayden has been at work for the last month, and while encountering most exasperating delays as the result of tardy transportation and accidents to the unused machinery, which have necessitated repairs, seems to have put everything in first class working order. Two trial runs have been made for the benefit of residences and the street service. The imperfections disclosed have been remedied as far as possible, and it is confidently expected that electrical service this year will be better than for several years.

The "Water Works"

In 1898, the franchise for "water works" was awarded to L.T. Yoder of Mt. Lake. The Park Water and Light Company was organized by Mr. Yoder. The first of several sources of water was the Crystal Spring. As we can see from the advertisement in this section, the Park Water and Light provided "turn-key" service for water and sewer, including installing the plumbing and appliances in your home.

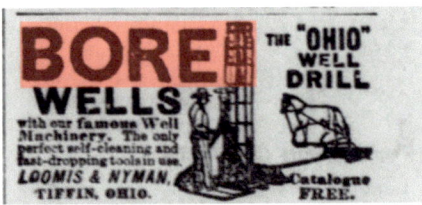

Jan. 22, 1892 Republican Advert for Well Boring Machine.

Surprisingly, just like electric service, the "water works" initially only operated during the summer.

From The Republican, April 7, 1898

> *"The (franchise) agreement on the part of the Association is to give Mr. Yoder control of Crystal spring and one acre of ground nearby where he will excavate for the purpose of gathering a supply of water.*
> *At this point a large steel tube will be sunk into the earth and the water allowed to accumulate from the spring. He will install a pumping engine which will force the water from the steel tube to a stand pipe to be erected on the highest point of ground within the limits of the Park and from which the water will be distributed to those who desire it by gravation. The capacity of the stand pipe will be something like 30,000 gallons and will be made of steel set on a foundation of masonry."*

> A force of men is putting in the water works at Mountain Lake Park. W. A. Liller, of Keyser, West Va., has the contract for the erection of the engine and pumping house. W. E. Landon, of Pittsburg, is putting up the stand pipe and laying the pipe.

From the Republican June 2, 1898

The water works provided by Mr. Yoder was highly anticipated but it appears to have had major problems in delivering the water. Many hotels and homes that subscribed to the water works were left with either "bad" water or no water at all. The first water "pipes" were made of wood; these actually performed better than the next pipe material, which was Terra Cotta tile pipe. (This type of pipe was subsequently used for sewer lines in the park.) In the summer of 1901, when the terra cotta pipes were used, one of the pipes burst under the pressure and left the Park "high and dry" for most of the summer season.[4] Several lawsuits were filed against the water works as people attempted to recover their costs for hauling water during the summer.[5]

Wooden "Pipe" similar to those first used in Mt. Lake. Courtesy Alleghany County History Museum.

Retrieved from Yodernewsletter.org

Terra Cotta Pipe laid out, to be installed underground. ca. 1900. In front of the Casino in Loch Lynn, Photo courtesy of Cumberland County Historical Society, A.A. Line Collection.

"Sewer Lines"

The installation of sewer lines seemed to proceed a bit smoother, and enabled indoor "necessary rooms". The pipe used was the aforementioned terra cotta pipe, some of which is still in use in Mt. Lake Park today. Of course, sewer treatment as we know today did not exist: the terra cotta pipes were simply run down to the Little Yough; swimming, wading or fishing would be an unpleasant experience downstream of the Park.

Electric, Water, & Sewers, Oh My!

During the past week sewer pipe was laid in the alley east of I street and extended to the Little Yough. This week the pipe is being laid in the alley east of F street extended. When this section is completed, work will commence in the Cozy Row section. Next season **two-thirds** *of the Park will be free from* **earth closets** *and be connected with the sewer system. The Park is to be put in the best sanitary condition possible.*
From the Republican Dec. 20, 1900.

A.D. Naylor Plumbing Crew, 1910 Photo and write up below from the Feb.-9, 1961 edition of the Republican. *"The name of the horse was Queen".*

The five men shown in the wagon constituted the plumbing crew of A. D. Naylor and company, and were enroute to some long forgotten job when they were snapped by an itinerant photographer. On the front holding the reins, is Will Cleveland, while sitting to his right is Ernest Bush. In the center is Will Lawton, while Tom Compton and Grover Stemple are perched on the tail gate, Stemple on the right. Not to slight the horse, her name was "Queen." S. T. Naylor, who supplied the picture, said the horse and its conveyance were furnished the men to drive to and from jobs located out of walking range.

The building in the background is the Bashford Amphitheater. The wagon appears to be heading east on Arbutus Drive.

In subsequent years, Mr. Yoder secured a different source for the "water works", over near Loch Lynn Heights. There were many hiccups along the way and many hotel and boarding house operators felt compelled to maintain their own water sources and storage. Even as late as 1920, well past Mr. Yoder's time, the lack of water supply was identified as the reason the Assembly house fire spread out of control and destroyed several buildings.

This brings us to our next Chapter: Calamities.

17 - CALAMITIES

As we have researched this book, we have invariably found news of several mishaps, petty thefts, fires and floods, and the like. In this, Mt. Lake Park was like anyplace else: things happened.

Here we will provide just a small number of the items we encountered.

The "First Accident".

> **An Accident at Mountain Lake Park.**
>
> The first accident in all the building operations at Mountain Lake Park, occured Tuesday last, in the falling of a scaffold at the "Auditorium." There were three persons on the scaffold at the time, and all were more or less injured. Mr. Joseph Painter was slightly injured internally, Mr. Jas. A. Enlow received a cut on the face and severe bruises on the hip and arm, and Bud. Wolf, aged about 13 years, son of Mr. Samuel Wolf, had his left leg broken below the knee. All are residents of Oakland.

The Republican July 1, 1882

Really the first accident?
—On Tuesday of last week while workmen were engaged on Dr. Logan's cottage, at Mountain Lake Park, a hatchet was accidentally dropped; by one of the men, striking Mr. Donald on the head and back, inflicting two ugly gashes. Dr, McComas dressed the wounds, and the patient is now able to work.
The Republican April 29, 1882

Mr. Burley's Horse Team frightened by Locomotive

> Mr. Burley's team was frightened by a locomotive while they were unloading a car load of lumber. They ran up the hill some distance strewing the lumber, uncouppled the wagon, then turned and crossed the railroad near Mrs. Car's, went up F street and through the wire fence near the office, where they were stopped.   J. A. E.

The Republican Oct. 11, 1884

Runaway horses were often a problem at the park. Mr. Burley from Moundsville was a builder. He also constructed the dam for the lake.

Horse Team and Carriage at Mt. Lake Hotel

Calamities

Bad Accident at the Park.

While Mr. Adam Howell, proprietor of the new hotel at the Park, known as the Columbian hotel, was engaged in unloading a large crate of crockery Monday morning the wagon started backward down the hill and caught him between the wheels and the building. His left arm was broken in two places, some ribs crushed and he was badly hurt about the back. He was in an unconscious condition for several hours and his life despaired of, but at this time he is resting quite easy and it will take a long time for him to recover.

The Republican July 20, 1893
This was when Jennie Smith's Brother-in-Law was just opening the Columbian hotel.

Robbery! The Republican June 7, 1894

Unknown parties affected an entrance into the depot at the Park last Thursday night and robbed it of $5 in cash, broke open two trunks and destroyed the telegraph instruments. There is no clue to burglars.

Mt. Lake Train Accident Jan 28, 1897 Wheeling Intelligencer

There were many accidents at the Mt. Lake – Loch Lynn railroad crossing over the years. This story from the Wheeling paper tells of an accident involving a black man who worked for Mr. Alderson.

Monday morning. Charles Washington. a (black) man in the employ of Major Alderson, left home with the major's horses hitched to a sled, to haul hay. To protect himself from the severe cold, Washington had wrapped his head in a scarf. He reached the railroad track at the depot at the time when No. 47 was due. Not hearing the whistle of the engine, Charlie drove on. Just as he entered the west-bound track the engine struck the horses and knocked them many feet ahead on either tide of the track; instantly killing the horses. and tearing the sled to pieces. and throwing Washington out, without hurting him.

Teamsters on the loose, 1900.

The Park must have appeared as one big construction zone during the off seasons. Here we have an issue with teamsters driving across folk's lots.

A warrant has been sworn out against some teamsters for driving across lots. The Association is determined to break up this bad practice.

The Republican Dec. 6, 1900.

Calamities

First Auto Accident?

As soon as there were automobiles, there were accidents. The car in the article below was apparently trying to ascend the hill over in Loch Lynn when trouble occurred.

The Machine Ran Away.

Mr. Cormay's locomobile which, by the way, was the first machine of its kind seen in this section, is with us no more. It is now in a repair shop or maybe a scrap heap somewhere. Sunday afternoon the owner, accompanied by a friend, attempted to mount Loch Lynn with the machine. As is usual in such cases the machine balked when about half way up the precipitous incline. The driver reversed the machinery hidden in the depths of the box intending to back down and take another start. This undone the operator and incidentally, also, the machine. The gear chain slipped from the sprocket wheels and a mad race down the roadway, backward at that, took place. Fate handicapped the race as a deep ditch was encountered into which the 'mobile piled upsetting it and knocking it into smithereens. The occupants were not seriously injured. The machine was loaded on a car Monday and sent east.

The Republican Aug. 29, 1901

Photo Courtesy Diana Runyon.

The Horses Keep Running, 1903

In Loch Lynn Heights last week a team belonging to Mr. Edward O'Donnell ran away with his little grandchild in the wagon. At imminent risk to himself Mr. Geo. Reckley caught the frightened horses and was dragged over one hundred feet before he succeeded in bringing them to a stop near Callis' blacksmith shop.

The Republican April 9, 1903

And Running, 1905

In a Runaway Accident Tuesday Night on the Mt. Lake Road.

Dr. Benj. F. Selby, of Oakland, was painfully injured Tuesday night about ten o'clock by his horse running away and throwing him from the vehicle to which it was attached.

In coming toward Oakland the horse stumbled near Oak Hall and in doing so disarranged some of the harness which allowed the vehicle to crowd it and caused it to make a bolt. Dr. Selby succeeded in getting control of the horse however when it, started to kick and again bolted. Near the turn of the road at Broderick's ice house the doctor was thrown into the road and fell upon a rock with his knee which caused a dislocation and probable fracture of one of the bones.

Shortly afterward the injured man was brought into town and taken to the McComas Sanitarium where he received surgical aid and is resting

The Republican Sept. 28, 1905. Dr. McComas to the rescue, again.

Calamities

MOUNTAIN LAKE PARK SUFFERS LOSS BY FIRE

New Association Building Used for Postoffice and Store Destroyed.

LOSS WILL AGGREGATE $8,000

Postmaster Rudisill Saved His Records By Having Them at His Home—Martin & King, Loose Heaviest—Building Insured for $2500.

This Nov. 27, 1907 fire which destroyed the Post Office was described as the most serious to date. It would set off an unfortunate chain of events for Mr. South Preston of Fairmont; he had invested other people's money in a couple of ventures in Mt. Lake and things did not go well.

Mr. South Preston, from W.Va., borrowed $1200 from Mrs. Lydia Strum and nearly $1000 from others to make a new start in the Park. The post office fire and bad business conditions caused Mr. Preston to lose everything and to "lite out" for New York.

The Jan. 16, 1908 Clarksburg Telegram picks up the story, describing Mr. Preston's, and his creditor's, misadventure in Park:

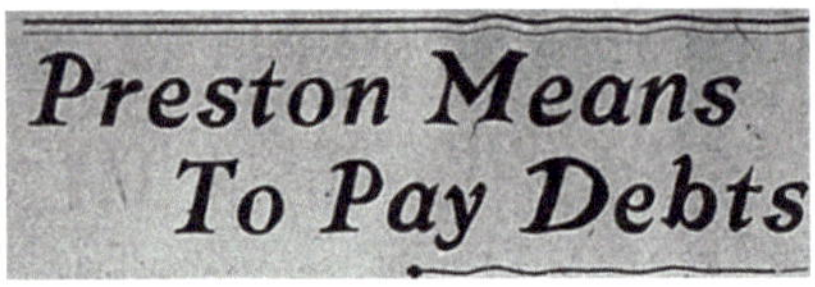

Preston Means To Pay Debts

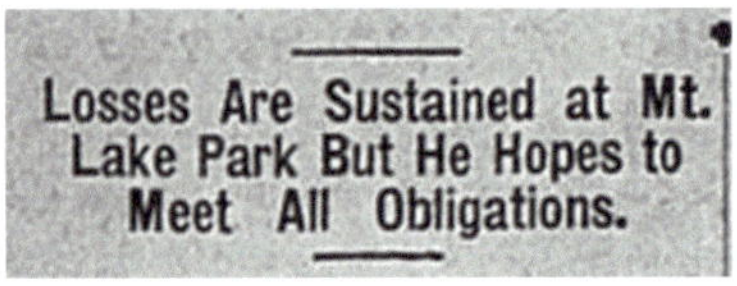

Losses Are Sustained at Mt. Lake Park But He Hopes to Meet All Obligations.

After preaching at Boothsville for two years and finding it not expedient for him to seek entrance into the conference as a traveling preacher, he decided not to ask for work this fall, but instead to go into business at Mt. Lake Park. While on that circuit he frequently discussed his plans with the people with whom he came in contact. When he borrowed money of Mrs. Lydia Sturm, of Enterprise, he explained to her what he wanted the money for, and invited her to go with him to Mt. Lake Park and see the house he intended to rent.

Last spring he moved to Mt. Lake Park where he leased, the Allegheny House, another boarding house, bought two cottages and started a store in the post office. He intended to start a newspaper there and would probably have done so had he not been discouraged by L. P. Carr, of Fairmont, who is familiar with conditions at the Park. Herscel Yost, of Fairmont, clerked in the store which was started in the post office.

From Mr. Preston's 1901 book, The Secret of Hamlet.

The season was a bad one at Mt. Lake Park. All the boarding houses lost money. This was sufficient put him in financial straits, but upon it all came the burning of the post office and the destruction of his store.

The story continues, stating that Mr. Preston planned to pay off his debts and return to the Park. We searched around but we did not find any other information regarding Mr. Preston's return to the Park. This should have served as a cautionary tale for other would-be entrepreneurs lured by the summertime crowds of the Park.

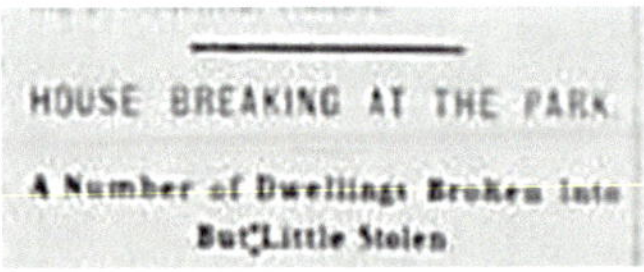

HOUSE BREAKING AT THE PARK

A Number of Dwellings Broken into But Little Stolen.

The Republican Mar. 5, 1908.

In a **1908 house break-in spree**, many houses were broken into but little was stolen. Among the Cottages entered were the Maxwell, Clayton, and others, including Felty's Store. The burglar was detected when someone noticed a lamp on in the Maxwell Cottage, during the off-season. This was noticed from across the way in Loch Lynn. The would-be thief was caught but later escaped. **Felty's Store**

Calamities

SECOND SERIOUS FIRE AT MOUNTAIN LAKE PARK

Association's Ice House Burned to the Ground Tuesday Morning.

THREE CARS ALSO CONSUMED

Which Stood on the Siding Near the Burned Building—Loss to Association a Severe One—Much of the Ice Will Be Saved.

The Republican June 11, 1908.

In June of 1908 another fire completely destroyed the **Ice House**. This fire was deemed to be of suspicious origins, but there was also speculation that the sawdust used when packing the ice could also be a contributor. The ice house was full of ice for the coming season; the ice was salvaged. We can only imagine the sight of all that ice in the smoldering ruins of the ice house. The ice houses burned down at least two times, perhaps, three. Each time it was rebuilt.

With the emergence of electric, new hazards presented themselves. The headline below describes a **near-disaster** at the **Amphitheater.** This occurred in August of 1910, after a show. Quick thinking by W.L Davidson averted disaster. The fire from "crossed wires" burned up a wall in the basement of the building. Davidson apparently put the fire out with water.

Ca. 1902. Photo from A.A. Line Collection Cumberland County Museum

LARGE AUDITORIUM ON FIRE

Crossed Wires Started Blaze and Structure May Have Been Destroyed.

Only by the timely discovery of a fire in the basement of the large auditorium at Mountain Lake Park on last Friday night, caused by crossed electric wires, was the building saved from total destruction, and the loss of many thousands of dollars averted.

The Republican Aug. 25, 1910

In addition to people and animals getting hit by the trains, occasionally a **train** would just **wreck** near the Park.

1912 Train Wreck Stanley Wood, at right. Courtesy Kevin Callis.

Wreck at The Park.

Monday morning about five o'clock a freight wreck occurred at Mountain Lake Park which blocked the west bound track for several hours and interferred with the movement of trains to a great extent. The cause of the wreck was the displacement of a portion of a large steel hopper which fell upon the rail and wedged itself in the switch points, derailing three or four cars and tearing up the track from a point near the operators' tower to the west end of the platform at the Park.

July 24, 1913, The Republican

1914 Theft at Maryland Home!

Evidently, the Park was not immune from small-time theivery. We imagine this theft was no small calamity for the workers whose wages were stolen. With all the comings and goings, and human nature being what it is, it is possible this type of petty-theft might have been more common than we might think.

> Saturday about 11.00 a. m. some one entered the room of the help of the Maryland Home and opened the trunks and suit cases and stole all the money found in them, which consisted of the wagas paid them, a few days previous. The theif has not been discovered.

The Republican Sept 3, 1914.

The Mountain Lake Community (distinct from the association) was granted the power to appoint **peace officers** as early as 1890, but this was opposed by the Association leaders. It was several years before this came to pass; some of the early policeman or constables were: Levi Echard, 1897, Thomas Callis, 1914, and B.C. Harmison, 1915.

> The annual committee have elected Mr. B. C. Harmison policeman and he has entered upon his duties.

Halloween Mischief

It's a good thing the police force was active by 1916, with the Halloween mischief going on that fall.

> But little mischief was done Hallowe'en night. A few wagons were placed on the board walk and Chas. Bunce's buggy was put in front of the post office door.

The Republican Nov. 2, 1916

Floods

"I am sorry the word 'Lake' was ever incorporated into the place." **Rev. John Thompson, 1892.**[1]

The Republican Aug. 16, 1884

> The dam at the lake partially gave way to the large volume of water last week, but it is again in good repair.

Most of the Park is situated on relatively high ground, but the area near the Little Yough was subject to flooding, especially when the dam at the Mountain Lake gave way. When that happened, the boardwalk would become flooded and the water could rise to nearly where the Town Hall is now located. It would also flood the Rathburn Planing Mill, on the other side of the railroad tracks in Loch Lynn Heights.

Calamities

PARK ELECTRIC PLANT ROBBED

Thieves Entered Building and Carried Portion of Machinery Away

One of the more unusual robberies inflicted on the Park was the 1919 **Great Power Plant Robbery**. Believe it or not, in 1919, the Power Plant was still only operated during the summer. Mr. B.F. Harvey had just fired up the power plant the week before, on June 5, 1919, and he managed to get everything in working order. But one week later, someone broke into the plant, which was located just below the dam at the lake, and they stole the "exciter" from the power generator. There was speculation that whoever stole the $300 part may have thrown it into the lake. There followed some discussion about draining the lake to try and find the part but it is not clear if that was attempted. One week later, the part was still missing, and this little request appeared the June 19 edition of the Republican paper:

> It is gratly hoped that whoever borrowed a part of our electric light plant, will return it so we can have lights again.

We can find no record of what subseqently happened, if the part was located or another part ordered, etc.

CONFLAGRATION OF PROPORTIONS SWEEPS MT. LAKE PARK

Five Buildings Entirely Destroyed and Numerous Others Damaged.

Fire about ten o'clock yesterday morning completely destroyed five buildings at Mountain Lake Park and damaged a number of others to a more or less extent, entailing a loss that at this time cannot be estimated, but it run well up in the thousands of dollars.

As mentioned earlier in the book, one of the worst fires ever experieced was the **Assembly House fire** in 1920. Not only did the Assembly house burn, but four other cottages next door burnt as well. The fire started when some men were burning leaves and embers blew under the porch of the Asseembly house. The sparks from the blaze ignited roofs and buildings several blocks away. Some of the other buildings damaged were the Ampitheater, the James Enlow Cottage, (now known as the Maggie Watson), and the Sincell Cottage (these last two are on H street).

MOUNTAIN DEMOCRAT, OAKLAND, MD., THURSDAY, AUG. 28, 1941

Historical Land Mark Destroyed By Fire At Mtn. Lake Park

The last calamity we shall cover, which is a bit out of our timeframe, was the 1941 **Tabernacle fire**. Jared Young of the Mt. Democrat had an extensive write up on the disaster. The origin of this fire was never established. The fire was quickly discovered by Mr.W.O. Bitzner, who lived nearby, in a cottage on Cozy Row; he saw the smoke, and tried to put it out. Fire departments were summoned but there was an issue getting a solid stream of water from the fire hydrant. Fire fighters from Oakland and Kitzmiller arrived on the scene but it was too late, the tabernacle was reduced to smoldering ashes. The tabernacle was subsequently rebuilt and the latest generation of it still stands today.

The fire that desroyed the Tabernacle increased the concern about a possible fire at the Amphitheatre. In 1946, the threat of fire would be used to justify tearing down the Amp. Many people lament the loss of the Amphitheater, but in the 1930s and 1940s, with the decline of visitors, the Ampitheater fell into disuse. We will cover this topic a bit more in a later chapter, when we examine the decline of the Park.

August 1941 Tabernacle Fire

Something that *might* instigate some calamities is depicted below. Taboo whiskeys, "for medical or other purposes," were just a short jaunt away in Oakland.

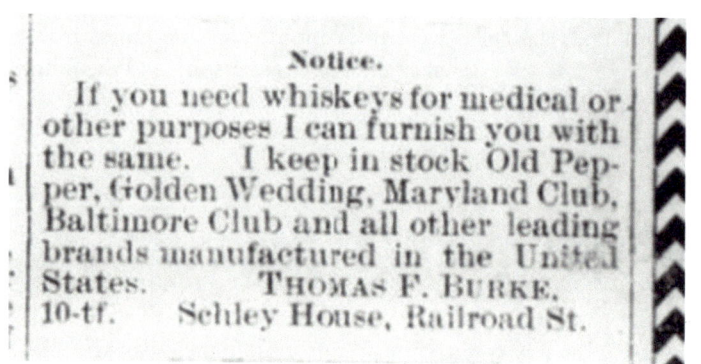

Notice.

If you need whiskeys for medical or other purposes I can furnish you with the same. I keep in stock Old Pepper, Golden Wedding, Maryland Club, Baltimore Club and all other leading brands manufactured in the United States. THOMAS F. BURKE.
10-tf. Schley House, Railroad St.

Advert The Republican, July 13, 1899.

18 - MORE ON THE FOUNDERS

Much earlier, we described some of early activities involved in creating the Mountain Chautauqua. We did not delve into the profiles of some of the founders at that time, because we didn't want to bog down the book just as we were getting started. We will provide some additional highlights here. This will be useful as the reader peruses the last chapter, "What Happened?"

Rev. Charles P. Masden

"Opportunity is a convenient time or favorable occasion, and, when once past, may never come again. Work at the right time, and everything assists you." **Rev. C.P.Masden**

Rev. Masden and the other Park founders certainly had great timing when it came to creating the Mountain Chautauqua; there was a convergence of the Camp Meetings, Temperance movement, the Chautauqua movement, combined with a new recognition of the value of purposeful leisure time.

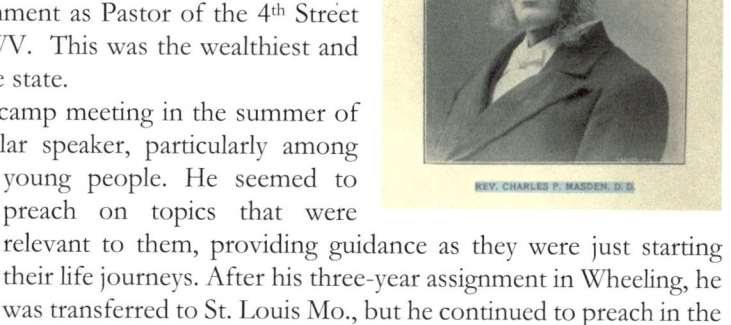

C.P. Masden was instrumental in driving the creation of the Park. He had traveled and preached at other "daughter Chautauquas", such as the one in Orange Grove, N.J. and he sensed the opportunity for a Mountain-based resort. Rev. Masden and Rev. Ryan are credited with the initial idea.[1] At the time of the founding of the Park, Mr. Masden was in the middle of a three year assignment as Pastor of the 4th Street M.E. Church in Wheeling, WV. This was the wealthiest and most influential church in the state.

Mr. Masden led the first camp meeting in the summer of 1882. He was a very popular speaker, particularly among young people. He seemed to preach on topics that were relevant to them, providing guidance as they were just starting their life journeys. After his three-year assignment in Wheeling, he was transferred to St. Louis Mo., but he continued to preach in the Park, and steer the association, of which he was an officer for many years. Dr. Masden built and maintained a cottage in the Park, this house would later be bought by Mrs. S.L. Allen and renamed Allenhurst. It was located on Oak Street. From the view in the Mt. Chautauqua illustration, the porch appears to have been overlooking Pleasant Valley. He bought and sold several lots during his connection with Mt. Lake.

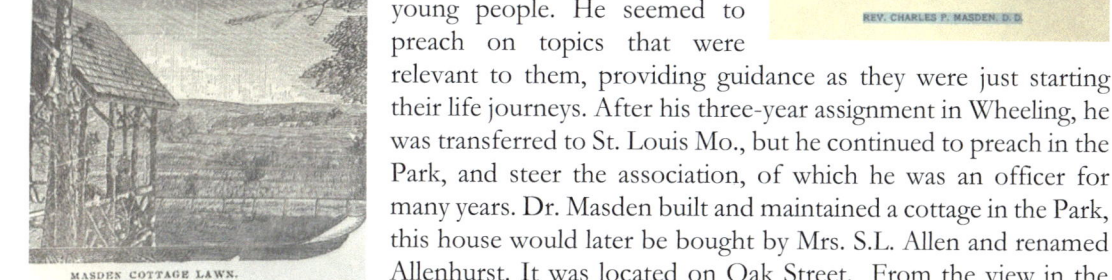

The Reverend was a contributor to the Christian Standard weekly, the periodical published by Rev. John Thompson (owner of the Deaconess Home) and Masden's essays were collected in his book, <u>Pentecost in Practical Life</u>, published in 1887.

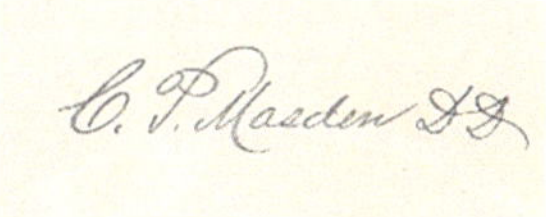

Rev. Masden and his wife, Laura, carried out assignments in different locales for many years, including a stint in Milwaukee, where he was known as "the marrying Parson"; this being due to the heavy demands of young people wishing to marry after traveling from nearby states and counties. Eventually the Reverend and his family settled in California. He died in Oakland, Ca. in 1930.

More on the Founders

Major Joseph Coleman Alderson

J.C. Alderson was a businessman and a parishioner in Rev. Masden's 4th Street church in Wheeling. Along with Rev. Masden, he saw the opportunity on the Mountaintop. The Major was the first Secretary of the Association and the very first minutes of their meetings are written out in his hand.

Mr. Alderson grew up in Alderson, Virginia (now West Virginia) where, as we can imagine, his family had a great deal of influence and were prominent in business. Mr. Alderson was a Major in the Confederate Army during the Civil war; served in the Virginia Calvary, was captured, and ultimately escaped. When offered a chance to take an oath of allegiance to the Union in exchange for freedom, Major Alderson declined. In his later writings, Major Alderson did not express a great deal of remorse about the rebellion.

For a time after the war, Major Alderson served in the U.S. Army in the west. He went on to run a successful insurance business in Wheeling.

From Confederate Veteran Magazine, 1912

Mt. Lake was not the only opportunity he saw in Garrett County. He was the founder who quickly purchased the land across the tracks and founded Loch Lynn, which he initially named "Lake View". His first wife, Mary Price Alderson, was the daughter of Samuel Price, Governor of West Virginia; she was responsible for the naming of Loch Lynn Heights and many of the streets, in honor of her Scottish heritage. Later on, Maj. Alderson owned and operated a farm in Loch Lynn. He was also one of the first builders in the Park; one of his houses is now located at the Northwest corner of Oak St. and E street. The home was initially located in the lot adjacent to its current location, but it was moved and extensively modified in the late 1950s. Major Anderson died in 1912.

Alderson Insurance Wheeling, WV. Courtesy of Carolyn Corley

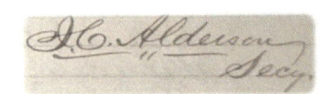

Rev. Edward W. Ryan

Rev Ryan was in the initial scouting party for the Park location and served as the first Vice President of the Association. After their look at Hoyes Pasture, it was Reverend Ryan who uttered the words: *"Brethren, this is foreordained for the place we are seeking,"* to which all in the scouting party agreed.

Mr. Ryan was the Presiding Elder of the M.E. Church, Wheeling District when the Park was founded. He built a cottage in the Park during the first summer of 1882. The Ryan cottage, now called Rosehaven, is located on G street.

More on the Founders

Mr. A.S. List

Ambrose Shaw List was a wealthy banker and businessman from Wheeling, West Va. Mr. List was the son of Henry K. List, a banker and business leader in Wheeling. A.S. List served as the first Treasurer of the Association and he served in that capacity through 1893. Mr List's daughter-in-law was Mrs. Lillian Blanche Creel (L.B.C.) List, the operator of both the grand Loch Lynn Hotel and the Overlook (Dennett) Hotel. Mr. List died in 1938.

AMBROSE SHAW LIST.

Solomon L. Allen

S.L. Allen, a merchant, hailed from Grafton, West Virginia; he was one of the first Directors of the Association. It is said that he and his wife, Laura V., were the first family to occupy their cottage in the summer of 1882. This house is still standing is now referred to as the Gables Cottage.[2]

In 1898, the Allens bought a cottage next door and four lots along Oak Street, from Charles P. Masden (this was the Masden Cottage)[3]. This house they named "Allenhurst". In the years around the turn of the century, this cottage served as a boarding house, where Mrs. Allen was assisted by Mrs. Reinhart, who previously operated the Park's Maryland Home. P.T. Garthright rented Allenhurst (as a boarding house) in 1904, and placed Mrs. Reinhart in charge of operations. In later years the house was converted to apartments. Allenhurst was destroyed by fire in 1955.

Allenhurst ca. 1900, Courtesy of Kevin Callis

Rev. James M. Davis

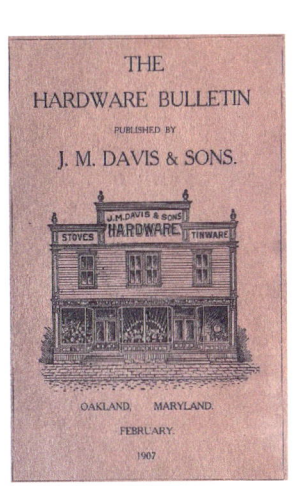

Mr. Davis was a preacher and influential Oakland merchant, instrumental in establishing the Association in Garrett County. Rev. Davis was "called into conference" with the Wheeling visitors and helped them create the Maryland association. (In order to establish the Md. Association, the founders needed several incorporators from Maryland.) Mr. Davis was one of the original shareholders and, starting in 1881, he served on the board as the first Superintendent of the Park. One of Davis' first assignments, in the fall of 1881, was to supervise the clearing of brush around the grove. One of his many ongoing winter-time duties was to manage the ice harvesting at the lake. In the 1890s, among other interests, Mr. Davis was a stockholder in the Mt. Lake Hotel Company. Other founders were shareholders of the hotel company as well, including Rev. Masden. Rev. Davis served as secretary and officer of the Association for more than 30 years.. He died in 1916.

THE HARDWARE BULLETIN
PUBLISHED BY
J. M. DAVIS & SONS.

OAKLAND, MARYLAND.
FEBRUARY.
1907.

J. M. DAVIS.

More on the Founders

Charles Wesley Conner

Charles W. Conner was a successful Wheeling merchant and one of the original shareholders of the Association. He supervised the initial construction of the dam and lake in the fall of 1882 and served on the board of directors from 1882-1904.[4] Mr. Conner built a house on the northwest corner of G and Cedar streets during that first summer of 1882. The house still stands today. Mr. Conner died in 1904.

The Conner Home ca. 1900, on G Street.

John Franklin Goucher

Dr. John Goucher was a widely admired proponent of women's education and a leading member of the Baltimore M.E. conference. In the fall of 1881, when the need to incorporate in Maryland became clear, the West Virginia founders invited Goucher, Rev. Charles Baldwin, and Rev. Van Meter, also of the Baltimore conference, to join them.[5] Goucher, one of the subsequent founders of the women's college that would become Goucher College, was enthusiastic and bought a large stake in the new association.

Mary & John Goucher, retrieved from Goucher College.

Clayton Cottage, 1906.

In 1883, he and his wife, Mary, purchased a cottage on I street from **Dr. Thomas Logan**. (Mr. Logan, from Wheeling, was himself another founder.) This cottage is often called "Clayton Cottage", named after U.A. Clayton, the man Goucher sold to in 1903. This cottage, greatly expanded, still stands today.

Over the years, Goucher acquired a near-majority stake in the Association and had a correspondingly large influence on the Association decisions. Although Goucher was a wealthy man, due in large part to his wife's wealth, he was not necessarily a successful business man. He and his wife were also heavily involved in the women's college (Goucher was named President in 1890) and other projects. It is said that Goucher's involvement in other far-flung projects, combined with the other board members lack of focus on the park created a kind of "absentee Landlord" syndrome and ultimately led to the financial demise of the Park. In 1920, with the Association deeply in debt, Dr. Goucher negotiated the sale of the Association to the Board of Foreign Missions. Dr. Goucher died in 1922.

More on the Founders

Charles Winterfield Baldwin

Charles Baldwin was a founding member of the Association, officer for more than 30 years, and President from 1883-1905. For more than 50 years he was a preacher for the M.E. Church, in the Baltimore Conference, serving many churches under the itinerant system of the Methodist denomination. Along with John Goucher, he was one of the founders of the Women's College of Baltimore (later renamed Goucher College). During his long affiliation with the Park, Rev. Baldwin led camp meetings, preached innumerable times, and was always well reviewed.

In 1882, he built the Baldwin cottage on the corner of M street and Youghiogheny Drive and owned this cottage for more than 30 years. This cottage is relatively small and is often identified as a quintessential "Cottage".

Dr. Baldwin remained active in the M.E. church throughout his life, preaching sermons well into his 90s. He died in Baltimore in 1938; he was 98 years old.

DR. C. W. BALDWIN'S COTTAGE

Yet another founder was Rev. Thomas B. Hughes. In 1882, he built Fernleigh Cottage, on E Street.

James A. Enlow

James Enlow, while not an early board member, was very involved in the establishment of the Park. Mr. Enlow rode out on horseback with the initial founders, surveyed the tract with Augustus Faul, and for many years chronicled the Park comings and goings in the Republican newspaper. He actually moved into a tent structure near the grove for the first summer of 1882 and carried out his duties as a "janitor". (This involved much more than what we think of today; he built many of the initial benches and outbuildings around the tabernacle.) After the turn of the century, Mr. Enlow purchased the "Maggie Watson Cottage". He, his wife, Alice, and family lived there for many years. Mr. Enlow was a relative of Ephraim E. Enlow, who expanded and named the Ruth Enlow Library. Mr. Enlow died in 1933.

Rev. Lewis A. Rudisill

In the late 1880s, and prior to engaging in the activities at the Park, Mr. Rudisill and W.L. Davidson helped organize the Topeka Chautauqua at Topeka, Kansas. At one point in 1890, Mr. Rudisill stopped by the Park on his way to preach at a camp meeting in Ohio; he was suitably impressed with the Park and, before he left, he was offered the job of business manager, which he accepted. Mr. Rudisill was the superintendent and business Manager for 13 years of the Park's heyday. He served in this capacity from 1890-1904. He oversaw many of the Park's improvements in the late 1890s, including the construction of the Hall of Philosophy, and the Bashford Amphitheatre and the enlargement of the lake. Mr. Rudisill was also the editor of the newspaper, The Mountain Democrat, for a number of years.

Signature from minutes, 1900.

His wife, Katie B. Rudisill, was active in the Park. She was President of the Women's Home Missionary Society, and one of the founders of the John Thompson Deaconess Rest Home.

The Rudisill's lived in a cottage they named "Unter-Walden", which means "Among the Oaks". This cottage, at the corner of F and Oak Streets, still stands.

19 - WHAT HAPPENED?

"Video killed the Radio Star" – **Madonna 1979**

As we bring this book to a close, it is now time to address a question that often comes up, and often quite early in discussions about Mt. Lake Park: *"What Happened? Why did all the activity stop?"*

The answer is deceptively simple -*the visitors stopped coming*. If we study other early places, their growth or failure is driven by natural resources, trees for lumber, coal for mining, etc. And if the timber played out, the people often moved on. In a sense, Mt. Lake's "natural resource" was its visitors. When they stopped coming, the events and businesses stopped as well.

Why the visitors stopped coming is considerably more complicated.

We can start by pointing out that there was a convergence of factors that drove the huge success of the Park, movements such as the temperance movement, the popularity of camp meetings, the availability of train travel at affordable prices, and the new notion of vacation and leisure time itself. All these factors made the Mountain Chautauqua assemblies a dramatic success. As Reverend Masden wrote in one of his sermons:

"Opportunity is a convenient time or favorable occasion, and, when once past, may never come again. Work at the right time, and everything assists you."

Rev. Masden later wrote in the same sermon:

"But if you work at the wrong time- let opportunity pass- you fail. Failure gives birth to failure and the opportunity is lost."

It is likely that new opportunities presented themselves after the turn of the century but the Association was not pre-disposed to changing with the times; they missed any new opportunities to continue their resort experiment.

Starting around 1906, there emerged a convergence of new events that impacted success of the Park; the Association did not adapt to the changing environment. Some of these factors and events are listed below:

- **Railroad subsidies** (the 10% rebates) and special excursion fares dried up. After a series of laws were enacted to limit monopolies and exclusionary pricing, including the Hepburn act of 1905, the rail roads stopped the 10 percent rebates to places like Mt. Lake.[1] This made it more difficult to continue to pay for "top-tier" talent.
- The **automobile** emerged as the preferred means of travel. The new car travel combined with bad mountain roads made it very difficult to travel to the Park. Vacationers suddenly had many choices and Garrett County meant "hard travelin'".
- **Mr. Rudisill and W.L. Davidson** "aged out" of their roles.

Fixing a Flat ca. 1914
Courtesy Garrett County Historical Society.

These two gentlemen were the drivers of securing the entertainment and "putting on the show". They had moved on by 1912. When W.L. Davidson resigned his position in 1912, the direct connections with the Lyceum Bureaus (talent bookers) were lost. In fact, on June 12, 1913, the Republican reported the following: *"So far the people are in the dark here as to whether there will be anything besides the Camp Meeting and the Missionary Meetings for 1913."* From 1914 through 1921, the Chautauqua Assembly was much smaller than the "Glory Days".

- **The Great War** (World War I)
  The disruptions to behavior and travel cannot be overstated. This continued from the outbreak of the war in the Spring of 1914 through the end of the war in 1918.
- **Spanish Flu**
  From the Spring of 1918 through the early months of 1919, the locals and visitors were rocked by the flu. 675,000 people died in the U.S including 100s of people in Garrett County.[2] All these deaths changed vacation patterns and routines.
- **Invention of Air Conditioning**
  By 1920s and 1930s, mechanized air conditioning began to make summers much more tolerable for the people that were drawn to the mountains because of the cool air. The new refrigeration also killed off Mt. Lake's ice harvesting business.
- Other Forms of Entertainment (**Radio, Moving Pictures**)
  To paraphrase Madonna, *"Radio killed the Chautauqua Star."* The emergence of radio entertainment in the early 1920s provided a wide range of shows, news, and religious programs that families could tune in to right from their homes.[3] Moving pictures were widely available in most towns and cities by 1920. This provided another means for enjoying shows and music without traveling to a Chautauqua or visiting a Vaudeville show.
- **Generational Change**
  The subsequent generations after the founding of the Park had been sent off to war, listened to shows in their homes, went to movies, and drove their cars where ever they wished to go. This younger generation's tastes changed and the Park was not the novelty that held their imagination. Even locally, the construction of the much larger Deep Creek Lake in the 1920s, with its secular bent and lack of tight "moral" restrictions became a very attractive option. *"Those young kids coming up were not interested in the Park and Camp meetings,"* recalled Ethel Turney.

  June 1, 1922 RCA Advert retrieved from en.wikipedia.org/wiki/RCA

- Finally, the economic **Crash of '29** and the ensuing **Great Depression**.
  Any hope of new improvement and growth in the Park collapsed with the Great Depression. Many of the wealthy Cottage owners lost virtually all of their assets and were left with only their "Cottage on the Mountaintop". These were dark days in the Country and in the Park. There are stories of formerly wealthy cottage owners moving into just a corner of their large cottages and "hunkering down".[4] At the same time, the collapse of the Chautauqua hastened the arrival of year-round residents and Mt. Lake's evolution to an actual town

What Happened?

The Association appears to start to show signs of financial stress just a few years after the turn of the century. In 1904, Mr. Yoder wrote a letter imploring the Board to "loosen up their hidebound laws" so that the Park might attract a wider clientele and continue to grow.[5]

This appeal fell on deaf ears. That same year, Mr. Goucher was concerned enough about the Park's prospects that he offered to sell his stock back to the corporation.[6] The Association did not buy the shares back and Mr. Goucher was left holding his shares until the Park was sold (by Goucher) to the Board of Foreign Missions.in 1920.

All the "ins and outs" of the end of the Association's business conditions are chronicled in the Mary Love book Once Upon a Mountiantop; we won't rehash them here. Suffice to say, the Park limped on after 1914, on through to 1920 when the Association, now $30,000 in debt, sold its assets to the Board of Foreign Missions.

There were great hopes for the Board of Foreign Missions to inject new energy and new money into the Park. The local citizens even raised money to help pay off the Association debt as a condition of the Foreign Missions' purchase of the Park.[7]

Shortly after the purchase went through, the Board of Foreign Missions declared that their charter, that of funding foreign missionary work, would not allow them to invest in improvements in the Park. The Park had a new owner but not necessarily an enthusiastic new owner.[8]

The following summers saw a substantial change in the focus of activities at the Park, more driven by locals and folks in the nearby region. The actual "Chautauqua" in 1921 lasted seven days with just a handful of performers.[9] The most significant activity in the Park in the Summer of 1922 program was…Sports![10]

The only surviving events were a shortened Camp Meeting and the occasional convention. An era was over, the days of the big Chautauqua Assemblies were gone. Many of the owners of the big Cottages continued to summer in the Park, but the crowds and entertainments were ever-dwindling. Eventually the Association's assets would be sold to other parties and, in 1931, Mt. Lake Park finally became an actual incorporated town.

Mt. Lake's full transition to a town and the events through the 1920s, 30s, 40s, and 50s will be left for another to chronical in yet *another* visit to the Mountaintop.

Mt. Lake Park Today

The Park today is a prospering community, with more than 145 buildings in the Mt. Lake Park Historic District, which is on the National Register of Historic Properties. Driving and walking tours are provided by the Park's Museum, located in the ticket office. The town also provides guided trolley tours during special events. Many homeowners take pride in actively restoring their properties; this does not often happen in a single episode, and is most often a bit of an ongoing activity.

As our current Mayor, Don Sincell, likes to say, *"It is the biggest town in the largest county in Maryland."* Most times it is a rather sleepy little town, except for a long weekend in July, when the town hosts a revival of sorts, the Mt. Lake Park Victorian Chautauqua Festival. Once again, the tents are erected, the platforms are set, the booked talent arrives, and more than 2000 visitors fill the streets. The festival typically hosts between 40-50 performers, many with a historic connection to the Park, and with several "acts" performing at the same time. The Mayor and Town Council are strong supporters of preserving the Park's history; they invite you to come visit, or to come and stay!

Source References

Chapter 1
[1] The Republican. (Oakland, Md.), 17 Sept. 1881
[2] There are numerous references in both the Republican paper and the Glades Star to the Electric being turned on and turned off. This summer-only electric happened from 1900 through 1919.
[3] Fowler & Kelly & Mountain Lake Park Association Of Garrett County. (1906) *Birds eye view of Mountain Lake Park, Garrett Co., Maryland*. Morrisville, Pa. [Map] Retrieved from the Library of Congress, https://www.loc.gov/item/75694539/.
[4] Example from Mt. Lake Park Messenger, 1884.
[5] Numbers found in 1896 Christian Standard.
[6] From 1892 Mountain Chautauqua.

Chapter 2
[1] The Glade Star Vol. 2, No. 8 March, 1952.
[2] The Hoyes of Maryland, by Captain Charles E. Hoye, 1942.
[3] The Hoyes of Maryland, by Captain Charles E. Hoye. 1942.
[4] Retreived from https://mht.maryland.gov/secure/medusa/PDF/Garrett/G-IV-B-007.pdf

Chapter 3
[1] The Republican. June, 30, 1938 Logan Carr's account of the formation of Mt. Lake Park.
[2] The Republican Jan. 20, 1927. J.A. Enlow's account of the search for MLP location.
[3] See Working at Play, A History of Vacations in the United States, by Cindy S. Aron, 2001.
[4] See Doctrines and Disciple of the Methodist Church, 1884. Paragraph 233.
[5] Mary Love audio interview with Ethel Turney ca. 1982
[6] From Association Meeting Minutes and news accounts.
[7] The Republican, Jan. 7, 1882.
[8] The Republican, April 28, 1938.
[9] The Republican July 20, 1916.

Chapter 4
[1] Retrieved from https://horseyhooves.com/horse-drawn-carriage-speed/
[2] For example time tables in the 1800s, see https://wx4.org/to/foam/maps/and_timetables1.html
[3] From Association Meeting Minutes.
[4] From Association Meeting Minutes.
[5] From Association Meeting Minutes.
[6] The Republican, June 5, 1891.
[7] The Republican April 1, 1882.
[8] From Association Meeting Minutes.
[9] The Republican Jan. 20, 1910.
[10] Mountain Chautauqua, 1896.
[11] From Association Meeting Minutes, 1882.
[12] 1887 Mt. Lake Marketing Flyer.
[13] The Republican, Sept. 11, 1902.
[14] The Glades Star, Vol. 4 No. 9, 1971.

Chapter 5
[1] The Republican, April 29, 1882.
[2] Mary Love Interviews, ca. 1882.
[3] The Republican March 10, 1938.

Chapter 6
[1] Per annotation in Town Hall.
[2] The Republican, Feb. 17, 1938.
[3] The Republican, June 11, 1911.

Chapter 7
[1] The Chautauqua Assembly Herald July 14, 1905.
[2] The Chautauqua Assembly Herald July 14, 1905.
[3] The Story of Chautauqua, by Jesse Lyman Hurlbut, D.D. 1921.
[4] The Chautauqua Assembly Herald July 14, 1905.
[5] Mt. Lake Messenger, 1884.

Sub chapter- Movers and Shakers
[1] The Christian Standard Periodical, 1896.
[2] See descriptions of the prayer sessions in The Christian Standard Periodical, 1896
[3] The Christian Standard Periodical, 1896.
[4] Ramblings in Beula Land, by Jennie Smith, 1887.
[5] Valley of Baca , a record of suffering and triumph., by Jennie Smith, 1880.
[6] Ramblings in Beula Land, by Jennie Smith, 1887.
[7] Association Meeting Minutes.
[8] The Republican July 5, 1894. Note that the date of death does not match her grave marker.
[9] The Republican Jan. 10, 1895.
[10] The Republican Aug. 10, 1899.
[11] The Republican Aug. 10, 1899.
[12] The Republican July. 27, 1899.
[13] The Christian Standard Periodical, 1896.
[14] Evening Star, Washington, D.C. March 5, 1915.
[15] The Republican April 8, 1915.
[16] From Mary Love audio interviews, ca 1982.
[17] The Republican Feb. 3, 1913. Ida Lee offering the book for sale.

Sub-Chapter – The Summer Schools
[1] By 1916, the Chautauqua Programs which were declining by 1914,were gone, with just some bible training and foreign Missionary work after 1916.
[2] Mt. Lake Messenger, 1884.
[3] Archives and Special Collections, Dickinson College, Carlisle, PA.
[4] Archives and Special Collections, Dickinson College, Carlisle, PA.
[5] From Cumberland County Historical Society, A.A. Line Collection.
[6] Archives and Special Collections, Dickinson College, Carlisle, PA.
[7] Retrieved from https://www.fi.edu/history-resources/kodak-brownie-camera#:
[8] From **Early Art and Artists in West Virginia**, page 194. by John A. Cuthbert, West Virginia University Press, 2000.
[9] The Republican, April 1, 1892.
[10] Retrieved from https://archive.org/details/kindergartenprimv27kind
[11] The Republican, Feb. 24, 1938.
[12] Mary Love audio interview with Betty Randol, ca 1982.
[13] Retrieved from https://archive.org/details/womanofcenturyfo00will

Sub Chapter – Chautauqua Performers
[1] See https://en.wikipedia.org/wiki/John_Wallace_Crawford
[2] From The Poet Scout by Jack Crawford,1879. Retrieved from conchohillsranch.com/captain-jack-crawford/
[3] Cumberland County Historical Society.
[4] The Republican, June 5, 1891.
[5] The Republican Aug. 6, 1900. Also see The Story of Chautauqua by Jesse Lyman Hurlbut, D.D.

Chapter 9
[1] See https://en.wikipedia.org/wiki/African_Methodist_Episcopal_Church
[2] See https://en.wikipedia.org/wiki/Methodism
[3] The Republican, Aug. 23, 1966.
[4] The Republican, Aug 27, 1903.
[5] Photo retreived from https://www.pbusa.org/202001-stan
[6] Fowler & Kelly & Mountain Lake Park Association Of Garrett County. (1906) *Birds eye view of*

Mountain Lake Park, Garrett Co., Maryland. Morrisville, Pa. [Map] Retrieved from the Library of Congress, https://www.loc.gov/item/75694539/
[7] The Republican, Sept. 20, 1906.
[8] Per 1920 Census.
[9] The Republican, June 28,1928. A sad story of Mariah Jones death.
[10] The Republican, Feb. 27, 1938.
[11] The Republican, June 11, 1914.
[12] The Republican, March 28, 1915.
[13] The Republican, June 15, 1916.
[14] See 1930 Census.

Chapter 10
[1] Association Meeting Minutes.
[2] The Story of Chautauqua by Jesse Lyman Hurlbut, D.D.
[3] The Republican, June 30, 1930. Dr. Logan Carr recalls.
[4] Mountain Chautauqua, April 1895.
[5] Retrieved from Ancestry. com
[6] The Republican, Jan. 8, 1920.
[7] The Republican Aug. 15, 1890.
[8] The Republican April 1, 1920.
[9] Association Meeting Minutes.
[10] The Republican, July 15, 1943.
[11] From Ed. Lewis' Recollections, Letter to Mary Love.
[12] See http://www.mtgretnatabernacle.org/about-us
[13] Retrieved from Findagrave.org. Posted by Timothy Metz
[14] See npcc 12165 http://hdl.loc.gov/loc.pnp/npcc.12165
[15] The Republican, Oct. 2, 1924.
[16] The Republican, April 6, 1961.

Chapter 11
[1] The Republican, Sept. 11, 1902.
[2] The Republican, March 31, 1883.
[3] Ramblings in Beula Land, by Jennie Smith, 1887.
[4] The Republican, June 5, 1913.
[5] The Republican, June 6, 1940.
[6] The Republican July 18, 1940.
[7] The Republican, June, 16, 1921.
[8] The Republican, June 10, 1941
[9] Courtesy of Garrett County Historical Society.
[10] The Republican, Dec. 14, 1889.
[11] See The Dairy Restaurant, by Ben Katchor, 2020.
[12] See https://restaurant-ingthroughhistory.com/2008/08/13/chain-restaurants-beans-and-bible-verses/
[13] From The Christian Standard, 1896.
[14] The Republican, Aug. 5, 1892.
[15] The Republican, June 26, 1902.
[16] The Republican, June 16, 1898.
[17] The Republican, May 18, 1893.
[18] The Republican, July 20, 1893.
[19] The Republican, Sept. 14, 1899
[20] The Republican July 1, 1882.
[21] The Republican July 20, 1916. Letter from Mrs. Thompson.
[22] From Mary Love audio interview with Ethel Turney., around 1982.
[23] Wheeling Daily Intelligencer, Jan. 28, 1897.
[24] The Republican, Dec. 5, 1901.
[25] Garrett County Schools of Yesteryear. Alice A. Feather Eary and Jean T. Williams Grose, 2008.

Source References

[26] As told to Marha Kahl in 1972.
[27] From Carolyn Henderson's notes.
[28] The Republican, June 1, 1911.
[29] The Republican June 13, 1907.
[30] The Republican June 1, 1911.

Chapter 12
[1] See https://en.wikipedia.org/wiki/Cottage
[2] From Ancestry.com
[3] See www.yodernewsletter.org for a detailed writeup on L.T. Yoder.
[4] Photo and some information from The Republican, March 1, 1951.
[5] The Republican March 1, 1951.
[6] The Republican, June 6, 1901.
[7] The Republican, March 9, 1916. Delegate Hayden had slipped on ice at the State House.
[8] Wheeling Sunday Register, April 24, 1887.
[9] From Maryland Land Records.
[10] Several points of information collected from Beverly Raily Robinson's paper on J.Sumner Stone,
[11] Glades Star, Vol. 5, No. 12, 2012.
[12] The Republican, July 12, 1900.
[13] From Photo inscriptions, E.R. Davis, Sr.
[14] From Karen and "Hop" Wooddell notes.
[15] See The History of Ritchie County, by Minnie Kendall Lowther, 1911.
[16] The Republican, Aug. 24, 1916.
[17] The Republican, Nov. 2, 1916.

Chapter 13
[1] From Association meeting minutes.
[2] The Republican, April 4, 1895.

Chapter 14
[1] The Republican, April 19,1884.

Chapter 15
[1] Courtesy of Kathy Malone.
[2] The Republican, Jan 8, 1903. There are many accounts of the summer-only electric, until 1919.
[3] The Republican, July 1, 1882.
[4] The Republican, Jan. 20, 1898.
[5] Retrieved from https://www.midcontinent.org/rollingstock/builders/tiffany.htm and https://en.citizendium.org/wiki/Refrigerator_car
[6] The Republican, June 11, 1908.

Chapter 16
[1] The Republican, June 15, 1894.
[2] The Republican, Nov. 21, 1901.
[3] The Republican, June 1, 1911.
[4] The Republican, July 25, 1901.
[5] The Republican July 10, 1902.

Chapter 17
[1] From Once Upon a Mountaintop, by Mary I. Love.

Chapter 18
[1] From the Wheeling Leader, Sept. 18,1881.
[2] The Republican, Jan. 20 1927.
[3] The Republican, Aug. 4, 1898.

[4] From Association meeting minutes.
[5] From Association meeting minutes.

Chapter 19
[1] See https://en.wikipedia.org/wiki/Hepburn_Act
[2] See https://www.cdc.gov/flu/pandemic-resources/1918-commemoration/1918-pandemic-history.htm
[3] See EH.net
[4] From Mary Love audio interviews.
[5] From Association meeting minutes
[6] From Association meeting minutes
[7] James Enlow recollections, Jan. 20, 1927.
[8] From Jared Young's writings in the Mt. Democrat and The Glades Star.
[9] The Republican, July 28, 1921.
[10] The Republican, June 29, 1922.

About the Author

George Cowgill spent his formative years in Deer Park, Maryland. He is an engineer and inventor, having been awarded more than 40 U.S. Patents. Mr. Cowgill earned a Master of Science Degree in Information Technology from Towson University in 2011. He is a lifelong history buff and he plans on writing another book on local history. He and his wife live in, you guessed it, Mountain Lake Park, Maryland.

Made in the USA
Columbia, SC
07 October 2024